Command the Network

A Practical Guide to Master Network
Configuration, Monitoring, and
Troubleshooting with Bash Scripts

Jeffrey Muniz

Table of Contents

Preface

In today's interconnected world, networks are the backbone of modern society. From global communication systems to enterprise infrastructure, the reliable operation of networks is paramount. As networks grow in complexity, the need for efficient management and troubleshooting becomes increasingly critical. This is where the power of Bash scripting comes into play.

"Command the Network" is your comprehensive guide to mastering network configuration, monitoring, and troubleshooting with Bash scripts. This book empowers you to harness the versatility of Bash, a ubiquitous scripting language available on virtually every Linux and macOS system, to automate tasks, streamline workflows, and gain deeper insights into your network.

Whether you're a seasoned network engineer, a system administrator, or a security professional, this book equips you with the knowledge and skills to:

- Automate routine network configuration tasks: Say goodbye to tedious manual configuration and embrace the efficiency of automated scripts for managing interfaces, routing, DNS, and firewalls.
- Proactively monitor network health: Gain real-time visibility into your network's performance by crafting scripts that monitor bandwidth usage, connectivity, and potential issues.
- Troubleshoot network problems effectively: Develop powerful diagnostic tools to quickly identify and resolve network problems, from basic connectivity issues to complex performance bottlenecks.
- Enhance network security: Implement security audits, intrusion detection systems, and automated security hardening scripts to safeguard your network.

This book takes a practical, hands-on approach. We start with the fundamentals of Bash scripting and essential networking concepts, building a solid foundation for you to explore advanced techniques. Throughout the book, you'll find real-world examples, code samples, and exercises to reinforce your learning.

By the end of this journey, you'll be able to confidently command your network with Bash, streamlining your workflow, improving efficiency, and ensuring the smooth operation of your critical infrastructure.

Who Should Read This Book:

- Network engineers and administrators
- System administrators
- Security professionals
- DevOps engineers
- Anyone seeking to automate network tasks and improve network management

What You'll Need:

- Basic understanding of networking concepts
- Access to a Linux or macOS system with Bash
- A text editor and a terminal emulator

We are excited to embark on this journey with you. Let's dive into the world of Bash scripting and unlock its potential for network mastery!

Chapter 1: Introduction to Bash Scripting

In this chapter, we'll lay the groundwork for your journey to network mastery. We'll explore why Bash is such a powerful tool for network management, set up your scripting environment, and dive into the fundamentals of the Bash language. Get ready to unlock the automation potential that lies within your fingertips!

1.1 Why Bash for Networking?

In networking, we often find ourselves doing the same tasks over and over again. Maybe you need to set up a bunch of new servers with the same network settings, or perhaps you have to constantly check if all your critical devices are online. Doing this manually, typing the same commands repeatedly, can get old fast. It's time-consuming, prone to errors, and let's be honest, a bit boring!

This is where Bash scripting comes in. Think of Bash as your trusty sidekick, ready to automate those repetitive tasks and free you up to focus on more interesting challenges. Bash (which stands for Bourne Again SHell) is a scripting language that lets you write a series of commands, save them in a file, and then execute them all at once. It's like having a superpowered command line!

Now, you might be thinking, "Why Bash specifically? Aren't there other scripting languages out there?" And you'd be right! Python, Perl, and Go are all great options. But Bash has a few key advantages that make it particularly well-suited for networking:

- It's everywhere: Bash is the default shell on almost every Linux and macOS system. This means you can write a Bash script on your laptop and it will likely run without any modifications on your servers, network devices, and even cloud instances. This kind of portability is incredibly valuable.

- It's powerful: Bash might seem simple at first glance, but it's packed with features. It has all the tools you need to interact with your network: you can run commands like ping, traceroute, and ssh, manipulate text, process data, and even control the flow of your script with conditional statements and loops.
- It's efficient: Bash scripts are incredibly fast. They execute commands directly within the shell, without the overhead of a separate interpreter. This makes them ideal for tasks that need to run quickly, like monitoring network performance or responding to network events.
- It plays well with others: Bash integrates seamlessly with other command-line tools. You can use it to pipe the output of one command into another, creating powerful chains of actions. This makes it easy to build complex network management workflows.

Let me give you a real-world example. Imagine you're responsible for a network with hundreds of servers. You need to make sure that all these servers have the latest security updates. Doing this manually, logging into each server and running updates, would take forever. But with a Bash script, you could automate the entire process:

Bash

```bash
#!/bin/bash

# List of servers to update

servers=("server1.example.com"
"server2.example.com" "server3.example.com")

# Loop through each server

for server in "${servers[@]}"; do
```

```
    echo "Updating $server..."

    ssh $server "sudo apt update && sudo apt
upgrade -y"  # Replace with appropriate update
command for your system

    echo "Done updating $server."

done
```

This script defines a list of servers, then uses a for loop to iterate through the list. For each server, it establishes an SSH connection and executes the update commands. This is a simple example, but it illustrates the power of Bash for automating network tasks.

With Bash, you can automate tasks like:

- Configuring network interfaces: Set IP addresses, subnet masks, and default gateways.
- Managing routing tables: Add, delete, and modify routes to control network traffic flow.
- Setting up DNS: Configure name resolution for your devices.
- Managing firewalls: Implement security policies to protect your network from unauthorized access.
- Monitoring network performance: Track bandwidth usage, latency, and packet loss.
- Troubleshooting network problems: Diagnose connectivity issues and identify bottlenecks.

And that's just scratching the surface! As you delve deeper into this book, you'll discover even more ways to leverage Bash for network management. You'll learn how to write scripts that are efficient, robust, and maintainable, turning you into a true network automation expert.

1.2 Setting Up Your Environment

Let's get your system ready for some serious Bash scripting action! The good news is that setting up your environment is pretty straightforward. You don't need any fancy or expensive software. In fact, you probably already have everything you need!

Here's the basic setup you'll need to start writing and running Bash scripts:

- **A Linux or macOS system:** Bash is the default shell in most Linux distributions (like Ubuntu, Fedora, Debian) and macOS. So if you're running one of these operating systems, you're good to go! If you're on Windows, don't worry! You have a couple of options:
  - Windows Subsystem for Linux (WSL): WSL lets you run a full-fledged Linux environment directly within Windows. This is a fantastic way to get a true Linux experience without the need for a virtual machine. You can install your favorite Linux distribution (like Ubuntu) from the Microsoft Store and access Bash from the Windows terminal.
  - Virtual Machine: You can also install a virtual machine (VM) on your Windows system and run a Linux distribution inside it. Popular virtualization software like VirtualBox and VMware Player are freely available. This gives you a completely isolated Linux environment to play with.
- **A Text Editor:** You'll need a text editor to write your Bash scripts. Remember, Bash scripts are just plain text files, so any text editor will do the job. But some editors offer features that make scripting easier, like syntax highlighting (which colors different parts of your code for better readability) and auto-completion (which suggests commands and variable names as you type). Here are a few popular choices:

- o Vim: A powerful and highly configurable text editor loved by many experienced programmers. It has a steep learning curve but offers unparalleled flexibility.
- o Nano: A simple and user-friendly text editor that's great for beginners. It's included by default in many Linux distributions.
- o Emacs: Another powerful and extensible editor with a rich ecosystem of extensions.
- o Sublime Text: A cross-platform editor with a clean interface and many useful features.
- o VS Code: A free and open-source editor from Microsoft with excellent support for various programming languages, including Bash.
- **A Terminal Emulator:** The terminal emulator is your gateway to the command line. It's where you'll run your Bash scripts and interact with your system. Most operating systems come with a built-in terminal emulator. On Linux, you might have GNOME Terminal, Konsole, or Xterm. On macOS, you have Terminal.app. On Windows, you can use PowerShell or Command Prompt, but if you're using WSL, you'll likely use the Windows Terminal.

That's it! You're all set to start your Bash scripting journey.

A Quick Test Drive:

Let's make sure everything is working correctly. Open your terminal emulator and type the following command:

```
Bash

echo "Hello, world!"
```

Press Enter. You should see the text "Hello, world!" printed in your terminal. This confirms that Bash is working as expected.

Now, let's create a simple Bash script. Open your text editor and type the following:

```Bash
#!/bin/bash

echo "My first Bash script!"
```

Save this file as my_script.sh. The first line, #!/bin/bash, is called a shebang. It tells the system that this is a Bash script.

Now, go back to your terminal and navigate to the directory where you saved the script. Use the cd command to change directories. For example, if you saved the script in your Documents folder, you would type:

```Bash
cd Documents
```

Next, you need to make the script executable. This tells the system that it's okay to run this file as a program. Use the chmod command to do this:

```Bash
chmod +x my_script.sh
```

Finally, run the script! Type:

```Bash
./my_script.sh
```

You should see "My first Bash script!" printed in your terminal. Congratulations! You've just written and executed your first Bash script.

With your environment set up and a successful test run under your belt, you're ready to move on to the next section, where we'll start exploring the core elements of the Bash language.

1.3 Basic Bash Syntax

Now that you have your environment set up, let's get into the nuts and bolts of Bash scripting. Don't worry, it's not as intimidating as it might sound! Bash syntax is quite straightforward, and with a little practice, you'll be writing scripts like a pro in no time.

Think of a Bash script as a set of instructions that you give to your computer. These instructions are written in a language that Bash understands – a language that's surprisingly close to the commands you type directly into your terminal.

shebang:

Every Bash script should start with a special line called the shebang. It looks like this:

```
Bash
```

```
#!/bin/bash
```

This line tells the system that this is a Bash script and that it should use the Bash interpreter to execute it. The #! is called a shebang (or hashbang), and /bin/bash is the path to the Bash interpreter. While it might seem like a small detail, this line is crucial for ensuring your script runs correctly.

Commands:

The heart of a Bash script is the commands it executes. These are the same commands you use in your terminal every day – ls to list files, cd to change directories, ping to check network connectivity, and so on. In a Bash script, you simply write these commands one after another, and they will be executed in sequence.

For example, let's say you want to create a script that lists the files in your current directory and then displays the current date and time. Here's how you would do it:

Bash

```bash
#!/bin/bash

ls -l

date
```

Save this as list_files.sh, make it executable (chmod +x list_files.sh), and run it (./list_files.sh). You'll see the output of both commands in your terminal.

Comments:

As your scripts get more complex, it's important to add comments to explain what your code does. Comments are lines that start with a # symbol. Bash ignores these lines when executing the script, so you can use them to leave notes for yourself or others who might read your code.

Bash

```bash
#!/bin/bash

# This script lists files and displays the date

ls -l  # List files in long format

date    # Display the current date and time
```

Variables:

Variables are like containers that hold information. You can store all sorts of things in variables – text, numbers, file names, and even the output of commands. To create a variable in Bash, you simply assign a value to it:

```Bash

my_variable="Hello, world!"
```

To access the value stored in a variable, you use the dollar sign ($) followed by the variable name:

```Bash

echo $my_variable
```

This will print "Hello, world!" to your terminal.

Quoting:

Quoting is important in Bash, especially when dealing with variables that contain spaces or special characters. There are three types of quotes:

- Single quotes ('): Treat everything inside the quotes literally.
- Double quotes ("): Allow variable substitution (replacing the variable name with its value) and command substitution (executing a command and using its output).
- Backticks (```): Used for command substitution.

Here's an example:

```Bash

name="John Doe"
```

```
echo 'Hello, $name!'  # Output: Hello, $name!

echo "Hello, $name!"  # Output: Hello, John Doe!
```

Strings:

Bash provides several ways to manipulate strings:

- **Concatenation:** You can combine strings using the +
  operator:

Bash

```
greeting="Hello"

name="Alice"

message=$greeting", "$name"!"

echo $message  # Output: Hello, Alice!
```

- **Substrings:** You can extract parts of a string using
  parameter expansion:

Bash

```
string="abcdefg"

echo ${string:0:3}  # Output: abc (extract first
3 characters)

echo ${string:3}   # Output: defg (extract from
4th character onwards)
```

- **String Length:** You can get the length of a string using #:

Bash

```
string="abcdefg"
```

```
echo ${#string}   # Output: 7
```

These are just a few of the basic syntax elements in Bash. As you progress through this book, you'll learn more advanced concepts like control flow (if/else statements, loops), working with files, and input/output redirection. But for now, you have a solid foundation to start building your first network scripts!

1.4 Variables and Data Types

Variables is one of the fundamental building blocks of any scripting language, including Bash. Think of variables as containers that hold information. They're like little storage boxes where you can put things like numbers, text, filenames, or even the results of commands.

In Bash, creating a variable is as simple as giving it a name and assigning a value to it. Here's how you do it:

Bash

```
my_variable="Hello, world!"
```

In this example, we've created a variable named my_variable and assigned the string "Hello, world!" to it. Notice that there are no spaces around the = sign. This is important in Bash!

Accessing Variable Values:

To access the value stored in a variable, you use the dollar sign ($) followed by the variable name:

Bash

```
echo $my_variable
```

This will print "Hello, world!" to your terminal.

Variable Names:

When choosing variable names, keep these rules in mind:

- Variable names are case-sensitive (my_variable is different from MY_VARIABLE).
- They can contain letters, numbers, and underscores.
- They cannot start with a number.
- It's a good practice to use descriptive names that indicate the purpose of the variable (e.g., server_ip instead of just ip).

Data Types:

Bash doesn't have strict data types like some other programming languages (like Java or C++). You don't need to declare the type of a variable beforehand. Bash treats all variables as strings, but it can perform operations on them as if they were numbers when needed.

Let's look at some examples:

```Bash
# String variable

hostname="my_server.example.com"

# Integer variable

port_number=80

# Floating-point number (treated as a string)

pi="3.14159"
```

Command Substitution:

One of the powerful features of Bash is command substitution. This allows you to capture the output of a command and store it in a variable. You do this by enclosing the command within backticks (```) or using the $(...) syntax:

Bash

```
current_date=`date`

# or

current_date=$(date)

echo $current_date
```

This will execute the date command and store its output (the current date and time) in the current_date variable.

Special Variables:

Bash has some built-in special variables that provide useful information:

- $0: The name of the script itself.
- $1, $2, $3, etc.: The first, second, third, and so on, arguments passed to the script.
- $#: The number of arguments passed to the script.
- $?: The exit status of the last command executed.
- $$: The process ID (PID) of the current shell.

These special variables can be incredibly helpful when writing dynamic scripts that respond to different inputs or conditions.

Real-World Example:

Let's say you want to write a script that pings a server and stores the result in a variable. Here's how you could do it:

```bash
Bash

#!/bin/bash

hostname="google.com"

ping_result=$(ping -c 4 $hostname)   # Ping 4
times

echo "Ping result for $hostname:"

echo "$ping_result"
```

This script pings google.com four times and stores the entire output of the ping command in the ping_result variable. It then prints the result to the terminal.

Exercises:

1. Write a script that creates two variables, first_name and last_name, and then prints a greeting message that includes both names.
2. Write a script that uses command substitution to get the current working directory and store it in a variable. Then print the value of this variable.
3. Write a script that takes a hostname as a command-line argument and pings it.

Understanding variables and how to work with them is crucial for writing effective Bash scripts. With this knowledge, you can start creating scripts that store and manipulate data, making your network management tasks more efficient and automated.

1.5 Operators

Think of operators as the tools you use to work with data in your scripts. They allow you to perform actions like comparing values, doing math, and manipulating text. They are essential for creating scripts that can make decisions, perform calculations, and automate complex tasks.

Bash provides a variety of operators, categorized as follows:

1. Arithmetic Operators:

These operators are used to perform mathematical calculations.

- +: Addition
- -: Subtraction
- *: Multiplication
- /: Division[1]
- %: Modulo (returns the remainder of a division)

Here are a few examples:

```Bash
a=10

b=5

sum=$((a + b))    # sum will be 15

difference=$((a - b))   # difference will be 5

product=$((a * b))   # product will be 50

quotient=$((a / b))   # quotient will be 2

remainder=$((a % b))   # remainder will be 0
```

Notice the use of double parentheses ((...)) for arithmetic operations. This is how you tell Bash to perform arithmetic evaluation.

2. Comparison Operators:

These operators are used to compare values. They return true (0) if the comparison is true and false (1) otherwise.

- **For integers:**
  - -eq: Equals
  - -ne: Not equals
  - -gt: Greater than
  - -lt: Less than
  - -ge: Greater than or equals
  - -le: Less than or equals
- **For strings:**
  - =: Equals
  - !=: Not equals
  - <: Less than (in lexicographical order)
  - >: Greater than (in lexicographical order)
  - -z: String is empty
  - -n: String is not empty

Here are some examples:

Bash

```
a=10

b=5

string1="hello"

string2="world"

[ $a -eq $b ]   # False

[ $a -gt $b ]   # True

[ "$string1" = "$string2" ]   # False

[ "$string1" != "$string2" ]   # True
```

```
[ -z "$string1" ]   # False
```

3. Logical Operators:

These operators combine multiple conditions:

- &&: AND (both conditions must be true)
- ||: OR (at least one condition must be true)
- !: NOT (inverts the truth value of a condition)

Here's how they work:

```
Bash

a=10

b=5

c=20

[ $a -gt $b ] && [ $a -lt $c ]   # True (a is
greater than b AND less than c)

[ $a -lt $b ] || [ $a -gt $c ]   # False (neither
condition is true)

! [ $a -eq $b ]   # True (a is NOT equal to b)
```

4. Assignment Operators:

These operators assign values to variables:

- =: Assigns a value to a variable
- +=: Appends a value to a variable
- -=: Subtracts a value from a variable
- *=: Multiplies a variable by a value
- /=: Divides a variable by a value
- %=: Calculates the modulo of a variable with a value

Examples:

```Bash
a=10

a+=5   # a is now 15

b="hello"

b+=" world"   # b is now "hello world"
```

5. Bitwise Operators:

These operators perform bit-level manipulations on integers. They are less commonly used in network scripting but can be useful in certain situations.

- &: Bitwise AND
- |: Bitwise OR
- ^: Bitwise XOR
- ~: Bitwise NOT
- <<: Left shift
- >>: Right shift

Real-World Example:

Let's say you want to write a script that checks if a server is reachable and if a specific port is open on that server. You can use a combination of comparison and logical operators to achieve this:

```Bash
#!/bin/bash

server="www.example.com"

port=80

if ping -c 1 $server > /dev/null 2>&1 && nc -z
$server $port > /dev/null 2>&1; then
```

```
  echo "Server $server is reachable and port
$port is open."

else

  echo "Either server $server is unreachable or
port $port is closed."

fi
```

This script first pings the server to check if it's reachable. Then it uses nc -z to check if the specified port is open. The && operator ensures that both conditions are true before printing the success message.

Exercises:

1. Write a script that takes two numbers as command-line arguments and performs all the arithmetic operations on them (addition, subtraction, multiplication, division, modulo).
2. Write a script that checks if a given string is a valid IP address (you can use regular expressions for this).
3. Write a script that takes a filename as a command-line argument and checks if the file is readable, writable, and executable.

Operators are fundamental to writing effective Bash scripts. By mastering these tools, you can manipulate data, make decisions, and create powerful scripts that automate your network management tasks.

1.6 Control Flow

Control flow refers to the order in which commands are executed in your script. By default, Bash executes commands line by line, from top to bottom. But what if you want to make your script smarter? What if you want it to make decisions based on certain conditions or repeat a set of commands multiple times? That's where control flow statements come in.

if/else Statements:

The if/else statement is like a decision-making tool in your script. It allows you to execute different blocks of code based on whether a condition is true or false. Here's the basic structure:

```Bash
if [ condition ]; then

    # Commands to execute if the condition is true

else

    # Commands to execute if the condition is false

fi
```

Let's break it down:

- if: This keyword starts the conditional statement.
- [condition]: This is where you specify the condition you want to test. We'll talk more about conditions in a moment.
- then: This keyword separates the condition from the code block that will be executed if the condition is true.
- else: This keyword (optional) introduces a code block that will be executed if the condition is false.
- fi: This keyword marks the end of the if/else statement.

Conditions:

The condition inside the square brackets ([ ]) is crucial. It's an expression that evaluates to either true or false. Bash provides various operators for constructing conditions:

- **Comparison Operators:**

- ○ -eq: Equals (for integers)
- ○ -ne: Not equals (for integers)
- ○ -gt: Greater than (for integers)
- ○ -lt: Less than (for integers)
- ○ -ge: Greater than or equals (for integers)
- ○ -le: Less than or equals (for integers)
- ○ =: Equals (for strings)
- ○ !=: Not equals (for strings)
- ○ -z: String is empty
- ○ -n: String is not empty
- **File Test Operators:**
  - ○ -e file: True if the file exists.
  - ○ -f file: True if the file exists and is a regular file.
  - ○ -d file: True if the file exists and is a directory.
  - ○ -r file: True if the file exists and is readable.
  - ○ -w file: True if the file exists and is writable.
  - ○ -x file: True if the file exists and is executable.[1]

Here's a simple example that checks if a file exists:

Bash

```bash
#!/bin/bash

filename="my_file.txt"

if [ -e "$filename" ]; then

  echo "The file $filename exists."

else

  echo "The file $filename does not exist."

fi
```

Loops:

Loops allow you to repeat a block of code multiple times. Bash provides two main types of loops:

- for **loop:** The for loop iterates over a list of items.

Bash

```
for item in list; do

  # Commands to execute for each item

done
```

For example, let's say you want to ping a list of servers:

Bash

```
#!/bin/bash

servers=("server1.example.com"
"server2.example.com" "server3.example.com")

for server in "${servers[@]}"; do

  echo "Pinging $server..."

  ping -c 4 $server

done
```

- while **loop:** The while loop continues to execute a block of code as long as a condition remains true.

Bash

```
while [ condition ]; do
```

```
  # Commands to execute while the condition is
true
```

```
done
```

Here's an example that counts from 1 to 5:

Bash

```bash
#!/bin/bash
```

```bash
count=1
```

```bash
while [ $count -le 5 ]; do
```

```bash
  echo "Count: $count"
```

```bash
  count=$((count + 1))
```

```bash
done
```

Real-World Example:

Let's say you want to write a script that checks the status of a web server. You could use a while loop to continuously ping the server and an if/else statement to display different messages based on the ping result.

Bash

```bash
#!/bin/bash
```

```bash
server="www.example.com"
```

```bash
while true; do
```

```bash
  ping -c 1 $server > /dev/null 2>&1   # Ping once
and suppress output
```

```bash
  if [ $? -eq 0 ]; then
```

```
    echo "Server $server is up!"

  else

    echo "Server $server is down!"

  fi

  sleep 5  # Wait for 5 seconds

done
```

This script uses $? to check the exit status of the ping command. If the ping is successful ($? -eq 0), it prints "Server is up!". Otherwise, it prints "Server is down!". The sleep 5 command pauses the script for 5 seconds before the next ping.

Exercises:

1. Write a script that takes a filename as a command-line argument. If the file exists, print its contents. Otherwise, print an error message.
2. Write a script that uses a for loop to create 5 empty files, named file1.txt, file2.txt, and so on.
3. Write a script that uses a while loop to continuously monitor the disk space usage and print a warning message if the free space falls below a certain threshold.

Mastering control flow statements gives you the power to write dynamic and responsive scripts that can automate complex network tasks. With if/else and loops, you can create scripts that make decisions, repeat actions, and adapt to changing conditions.

1.7 Working with Files

Files are an essential part of any operating system, and Bash provides a powerful set of tools for interacting with them. Whether you need to read configuration files, write log data, or manipulate network data, Bash has you covered.

Let's explore some of the most common commands for working with files in Bash:

1. cat (Concatenate and Print)

The cat command is primarily used to display the contents of a file.

Bash

cat my_file.txt

This will print the contents of my_file.txt to your terminal. You can also use cat to combine multiple files:

```
Bash
```

```
cat file1.txt file2.txt > combined_file.txt
```

This will concatenate file1.txt and file2.txt and save the combined content in combined_file.txt.

2. ls (List Directory Contents)

The ls command lists the files and directories in a given directory.

```
Bash
```

```
ls
```

This will list the contents of your current directory. Here are some useful options:

- -l: Displays files in long format (including permissions, size, modification time).
- -a: Shows all files, including hidden files (those starting with a dot).

- -h: Displays file sizes in human-readable format (e.g., KB, MB, GB).

3. cp (Copy)

The cp command copies files and directories.

Bash

```
cp my_file.txt my_file_copy.txt
```

This will create a copy of my_file.txt named my_file_copy.txt. To copy a directory, use the -r option (recursive):

Bash

```
cp -r my_directory my_directory_copy
```

4. mv (Move)

The mv command moves or renames files and directories.

Bash

```
mv my_file.txt new_location/
```

This will move my_file.txt to the new_location directory. To rename a file:

Bash

```
mv my_file.txt renamed_file.txt
```

5. rm (Remove)

The rm command removes files and directories.

Bash

```
rm my_file.txt
```

To remove a directory, use the -r option:

```Bash
rm -r my_directory
```

Caution: Be careful with rm, especially with the -r option. Deleted files are usually gone for good!

6. touch (Create Empty File)

The touch command creates an empty file if it doesn't exist. If the file already exists, it updates its modification time.

```Bash
touch my_new_file.txt
```

7. mkdir (Make Directory)

The mkdir command creates a new directory.

```Bash
mkdir my_new_directory
```

8. head **and** tail

- head: Displays the first few lines of a file.

```Bash
head -n 5 my_file.txt  # Display the first 5 lines
```

- tail: Displays the last few lines of a file.

```Bash

tail -n 10 my_file.txt  # Display the last 10
lines
```

tail -f my_file.txt # Continuously monitor the file for new lines

Real-World Examples:

- Reading Configuration Files: You can use cat or grep to read and extract information from network configuration files like /etc/network/interfaces or /etc/resolv.conf.
- Writing Log Files: You can use echo or printf to write messages and data to log files, helping you track network events and troubleshoot problems.
- Manipulating Network Data: You can use commands like cut, awk, and sed to extract, filter, and transform network data from files or command output.

Exercises:

1. Write a script that creates a new directory, copies a file into it, and then lists the contents of the directory.
2. Write a script that reads a log file and extracts all lines that contain a specific keyword.
3. Write a script that takes a filename as a command-line argument and appends the current date and time to the end of the file.

By mastering these file manipulation commands, you'll be well-equipped to handle a wide range of network automation tasks. You can manage configuration files, process log data, and create scripts that interact with the file system effectively.

1.8 Input/Output and Redirection

Let's talk about how Bash handles input and output, and how you can control the flow of information within your scripts. This might sound a bit technical, but it's actually quite intuitive. Think of it like plumbing – you have pipes that carry data from one place to another, and you can use various tools to redirect that flow.

Standard Streams:

In Bash, every command has three standard streams:

- Standard Input (stdin): This is where a command receives its input. By default, stdin is connected to your keyboard. When you type something in the terminal and press Enter, that input is sent to the command through stdin.
- Standard Output (stdout): This is where a command sends its output. By default, stdout is connected to your terminal screen. When a command produces output, it's displayed on your screen through stdout.
- Standard Error (stderr): This is where a command sends error messages. Like stdout, stderr is also usually connected to your terminal screen.

Redirection:

Now, the interesting part is that you can redirect these streams. You can send the output of a command to a file instead of the screen, or you can read input from a file instead of the keyboard. This gives you a lot of flexibility in how you handle data in your scripts.

Here are the most common redirection operators:

- >: Redirects stdout to a file (overwrites the file if it exists).

Bash

```
ls -l > file_list.txt
```

This will save the output of the ls -l command (the long listing of files) to a file named file_list.txt.

- **>>:** Redirects stdout to a file (appends to the file if it exists).

Bash

```
date >> log_file.txt
```

This will add the current date and time to the end of log_file.txt.

- **<:** Redirects stdin from a file.

Bash

```
wc -w < my_file.txt
```

This will count the number of words in my_file.txt by reading its content from the file instead of the keyboard.

- **| (Pipe):** Connects the stdout of one command to the stdin of another.

Bash

```
grep "error" log_file.txt | wc -l
```

This will filter the lines in log_file.txt that contain the word "error" and then count the number of filtered lines.

Here Documents:

Here documents allow you to provide input to a command directly within your script. This is useful when you need to feed multi-line input to a command.

```Bash
cat << EOF > my_file.txt

This is the first line.

This is the second line.

EOF
```

This will create a file named my_file.txt with the two lines of text specified within the EOF markers.

/dev/null:

/dev/null is a special file that discards any data written to it. It's like a black hole for data. This is useful when you want to suppress the output of a command.

```Bash
ls -l > /dev/null
```

This will execute the ls -l command, but its output will be discarded.

Real-World Examples:

- Saving Command Output: You can redirect the output of network commands like ping, traceroute, or nmap to files for later analysis or reporting.
- Creating Configuration Files: You can use redirection to create configuration files with specific content from within your scripts.
- Filtering Log Files: You can use pipes to filter and process log files, extracting relevant information or identifying error messages.

- Automating Backups: You can redirect the output of backup commands (like tar or rsync) to log files to keep track of backup operations.

Exercises:

1. Write a script that pings a server and saves the output to a file named ping_results.txt.
2. Write a script that reads a list of hostnames from a file and pings each hostname.
3. Write a script that filters a log file for error messages and saves the filtered lines to a separate file.

Input/output redirection is essential for writing efficient and flexible Bash scripts. By mastering these techniques, you can control the flow of data within your scripts, automate tasks more effectively, and create powerful network management tools.

1.9 Command-Line Arguments

Let's discuss how to make your Bash scripts more flexible and reusable by using command-line arguments. You see, when you run a script, you can provide extra information to it right there on the command line. This information can be anything – filenames, server addresses, numbers, options – you name it. These pieces of information are called command-line arguments, and they allow you to customize the behavior of your script without modifying the script itself.

Think of it like this: you have a script that pings a server. Instead of hardcoding the server address within the script, you can make it accept the server address as a command-line argument. This way, you can use the same script to ping different servers without having to edit the code every time.

Accessing Arguments:

Bash provides special variables to access these command-line arguments within your script:

- $0: This variable always holds the name of the script itself.
- $1: This variable holds the first argument you provide on the command line.
- $2: This variable holds the second argument, and so on.
- $#: This variable holds the total number of arguments provided.
- $@: This variable holds all the arguments as a list.
- $*: This variable also holds all the arguments but treats them as a single string.

Let's see an example. Save this script as greet.sh:

Bash

```
#!/bin/bash

echo "Hello, $1!"
```

Now, run this script with your name as an argument:

Bash

```
./greet.sh Alice
```

The output will be:

Hello, Alice!

Here, $1 within the script gets replaced with "Alice" because it's the first argument you provided on the command line.

Using Multiple Arguments:

You can use multiple arguments to provide more information to your script. For instance, you could modify the greet.sh script to accept both a first and last name:

Bash

```bash
#!/bin/bash

echo "Hello, $1 $2!"
```

Now, run it like this:

Bash

```bash
./greet.sh Alice Wonderland
```

And you'll get:

```
Hello, Alice Wonderland!
```

Checking for Arguments:

It's always a good idea to check if the user has provided the necessary arguments before proceeding with your script. You can use the $# variable and an if statement to do this:

Bash

```bash
#!/bin/bash

if [ $# -ne 2 ]; then

  echo "Usage: $0 <first_name> <last_name>"

  exit 1

fi

echo "Hello, $1 $2!"
```

This script checks if the number of arguments ($#) is not equal to 2. If it's not, it prints a usage message and exits with an error code (exit 1).

Real-World Examples:

- Network Scanning: You can write a script that takes a hostname or IP address as an argument and performs a network scan using tools like nmap.
- File Management: You can write a script that takes a filename as an argument and performs operations on that file (e.g., copying, moving, deleting).
- Log Analysis: You can write a script that takes a log file name and a keyword as arguments and searches the log file for that keyword.
- Backup Scripts: You can create a backup script that takes the source directory and destination directory as arguments.

Exercises:

1. Write a script that takes a hostname as an argument and pings it.
2. Write a script that takes two filenames as arguments and compares their contents.
3. Write a script that takes a directory name as an argument and lists all the files in that directory, including their sizes.

By using command-line arguments, you can create versatile and reusable scripts that adapt to different situations. This makes your scripts more powerful and saves you from having to write separate scripts for slightly different tasks.

1.10 Scripting Best Practices

Let's discuss how to write Bash scripts that are not only functional but also elegant, readable, and maintainable. Think of it like craftsmanship – you want to create scripts that are well-structured, efficient, and easy to understand, both for yourself and for anyone else who might work with your code.

Here are some best practices to keep in mind as you embark on your Bash scripting journey:

1. Use Comments Liberally:

Comments are your friends! They are lines in your script that begin with a # symbol. Bash ignores these lines when executing the script, so you can use them to explain what your code does, clarify complex logic, or leave notes for yourself or others.

Bash

```bash
#!/bin/bash

# This script checks the status of a web server.

server_address="www.example.com"

# Ping the server and suppress output.

ping -c 1 $server_address > /dev/null 2>&1

# Check the exit status of the ping command.

if [ $? -eq 0 ]; then

   echo "Server $server_address is up!"

else

   echo "Server $server_address is down!"

fi
```

See how the comments make the code easier to understand? Make it a habit to comment on your code as you write it. It might seem like extra work, but it will save you time and headaches in the long run.

2. Choose Meaningful Variable Names:

Use descriptive variable names that clearly indicate the purpose of the variable. Instead of using generic names like x or var, use names like server_ip, port_number, or log_file. This makes your code much more readable and self-documenting.

Bash

```
# Good

server_ip="192.168.1.10"

port_number=80

# Not so good

x="192.168.1.10"

y=80
```

3. Indent Your Code:

Use consistent indentation to visually structure your code and make it easier to follow the flow of logic. This is particularly important for if/else statements and loops.

Bash

```
# Good

if [ -f "$filename" ]; then

   echo "File exists."

else

   echo "File does not exist."

fi
```

```bash
# Not so good

if [ -f "$filename" ]; then

echo "File exists."

else

echo "File does not exist."

fi
```

4. Write Modular Code:

For complex scripts, break down the tasks into smaller, reusable functions. This makes your code more organized, easier to test, and less prone to errors.

Bash

```bash
#!/bin/bash

# Function to ping a server

ping_server() {

  ping -c 4 $1 > /dev/null 2>&1

  if [ $? -eq 0 ]; then

    echo "$1 is reachable."

  else

    echo "$1 is unreachable."

  fi

}
```

```bash
# Call the function with different servers

ping_server "www.google.com"

ping_server "www.example.com"
```

5. Handle Errors Gracefully:

Things don't always go as planned. Network connections can fail, files might not exist, or users might provide invalid input. Include error checking in your scripts to handle these situations gracefully.

Bash

```bash
#!/bin/bash

if [ -f "$filename" ]; then

  # Process the file

else

  echo "Error: File not found: $filename"

  exit 1  # Exit with an error code

fi
```

6. Quote Variables:

Always quote your variables, especially when they contain spaces or special characters. This prevents unexpected behavior and ensures that your script works correctly in all situations.

Bash

```bash
# Good

echo "$my_variable"
```

```
# Potentially problematic

echo $my_variable
```

7. Use the Right Tools:

Bash has a rich set of built-in commands and utilities. Choose the right tool for the job. For example, use cut to extract fields from text, awk for more complex text processing, and sed for text transformations.

8. Test Your Scripts Thoroughly:

Before deploying your scripts, test them thoroughly with different inputs and scenarios. This helps you identify and fix any bugs or unexpected behavior.

9. Use Version Control:

If you're working on larger projects or collaborating with others, use a version control system like Git to track changes to your scripts and manage different versions.

10. Keep Learning:

The world of Bash scripting is vast and ever-evolving. Stay curious, explore new commands and techniques, and continue to improve your scripting skills.

By following these best practices, you'll write Bash scripts that are not only effective but also robust, maintainable, and a pleasure to work with. Remember, writing good code is an ongoing process of learning and refinement. So keep practicing, keep experimenting, and keep improving!

Chapter 2: Essential Networking Concepts

Before we can start writing powerful Bash scripts to manage networks, we need to have a solid understanding of how networks actually work. Don't worry, I won't bore you with dry lectures and complicated diagrams. We'll keep things practical and focus on the concepts that are most relevant to Bash scripting for network management.

2.1 Network Fundamentals

A network is simply a collection of interconnected devices that can communicate with each other. These devices can be computers, servers, smartphones, printers, or any other device capable of sending and receiving data. The purpose of a network is to share resources, such as files, printers, internet access, and applications.

Think of your home Wi-Fi network. You probably have multiple devices – laptops, smartphones, maybe a smart TV – all connected to the same network. This allows you to share files between devices, print documents from any device, and access the internet from anywhere in your home.

Key Components of a Network:

- Network Interface Card (NIC): This is the hardware component that allows a device to connect to a network. It's like the "door" that lets your computer enter the network. Each NIC has a unique physical address called a MAC address (Media Access Control address).
- Physical Media: This is the medium through which data travels between devices. It can be physical cables (like

Ethernet cables), wireless signals (like Wi-Fi), or fiber optic lines. Think of it as the "roads" that connect the devices.

- Networking Devices: These are specialized devices that help manage and control network traffic. Some common examples include:
    - Hubs: Simple devices that broadcast data to all connected devices.
    - Switches: More intelligent devices that forward data only to the intended recipient.
    - Routers: Devices that connect different networks and forward data between them.
    - Firewalls: Security devices that control incoming and outgoing network traffic.
- Protocols: These are the "rules of the road" that govern how data is transmitted over a network. They define how data is formatted, addressed, transmitted, and received. We'll discuss some important protocols in the next section.

Network Models:

To understand how networks operate, we often use layered models. One of the most common models is the OSI (Open Systems Interconnection) model, which divides network communication into seven layers:

1. Physical Layer: Deals with the physical transmission of data over the network media (cables, wireless signals).
2. Data Link Layer: Handles error detection and correction, and provides access control to the physical media.
3. Network Layer: Responsible for addressing and routing data packets between networks.
4. Transport Layer: Provides reliable data transfer between applications, including error checking and flow control.
5. Session Layer: Establishes, manages, and terminates communication sessions between applications.
6. Presentation Layer: Handles data formatting, encryption, and compression.

7. **Application Layer:** Provides network services to applications, such as email, file transfer, and web browsing.

While the OSI model is a useful conceptual framework, the TCP/IP model (which we'll discuss later) is more closely aligned with how the internet actually works.

Understanding these network fundamentals gives you the context you need to write effective Bash scripts. When you write scripts to configure network interfaces, manage routing, or troubleshoot network problems, you'll be working with these underlying components and concepts.

For example, if you're writing a script to gather network information, you might use commands like ifconfig or ip to get details about the network interface card, or route to view the routing table.

Real-World Example:

Let's say you're troubleshooting a network connectivity issue. You might use the ping command (which relies on the ICMP protocol) to check if you can reach a remote server. If the ping fails, you might use traceroute to trace the path of the packets and identify where the connection is failing. These tools and techniques are all based on the network fundamentals we've discussed.

Exercises:

1. Use the ip a command to view the network interfaces on your system. Identify the MAC address of your primary network interface.
2. Use the ping command to test connectivity to a website (e.g., ping www.google.com). Observe the output and identify the IP address of the website.
3. Use the traceroute command to trace the route to a remote server (e.g., traceroute www.example.com). Analyze the output and see how many hops it takes to reach the server.

2.2 IP Addresses and Subnetting

An IP address is a numerical label assigned to each device connected to a computer network that uses the Internet Protocol[1] (IP) for communication. It serves two primary functions:

1. Host Identification: It uniquely identifies a specific device on a network.
2. Location Addressing: It helps to locate the device on the network and route data to it.

IPv4 Addresses:

The most common type of IP address you'll encounter is IPv4 (Internet Protocol version 4). An IPv4 address is a 32-bit number, usually represented as four decimal numbers separated by dots (e.g., 192.168.1.10). Each number ranges from 0 to 255.

IPv6 Addresses:

Due to the increasing number of devices connected to the internet, the pool of available IPv4 addresses is depleting. This led to the development of IPv6 (Internet Protocol version 6), which uses 128-bit addresses. IPv6 addresses are represented as eight groups of four hexadecimal digits, separated by colons (e.g., 2001:0db8:85a3:0000:0000:8a2e:0370:7334).[2]

While IPv4 is still widely used, IPv6 is gradually being adopted to accommodate the growing number of internet-connected devices.

Subnetting:

Now, let's talk about subnetting. Subnetting is the process of dividing a network into smaller, more manageable subnetworks. Think of it like dividing a city into different neighborhoods. This helps to:

- Improve Network Performance: By reducing the amount of traffic on each subnet.
- Enhance Security: By isolating different parts of the network.
- Simplify Network Management: By organizing devices into logical groups.

Subnet Mask:

Each subnet is identified by a subnet mask, which is a 32-bit number that tells you which part of the IP address identifies the network and which part identifies the host within that network. The subnet mask is usually written in the same format as an IPv4 address (e.g., 255.255.255.0).

How Subnetting Works:

Let's look at an example. Consider the IP address 192.168.1.10 and the subnet mask 255.255.255.0.

- The subnet mask 255.255.255.0 means that the first three octets (192.168.1) identify the network address, and the last octet (10) identifies the host address within that network.
- Any device with an IP address that starts with 192.168.1 is on the same network.
- The host portion (10 in this case) can be any number between 1 and 254 (0 and 255 are reserved for special purposes).

CIDR Notation:

CIDR (Classless Inter-Domain Routing) notation is a compact way of representing IP addresses and their associated subnet masks. It's written as the IP address followed by a slash and the number of bits in the network portion of the address (e.g., 192.168.1.10/24). In this example, /24 means that the first 24 bits of the IP address represent the network address.

When you write Bash scripts to configure network interfaces, you'll need to specify the IP address and subnet mask (or CIDR notation). You might also need to work with subnetting when writing scripts to manage routing tables or firewalls.

Real-World Examples:

- Configuring a Network Interface: When you configure a network interface on a Linux server, you'll typically use commands like ifconfig or ip to set the IP address and subnet mask. For example:

Bash

```
sudo ip addr add 192.168.1.10/24 dev eth0
```

This command assigns the IP address 192.168.1.10 with a subnet mask of 255.255.255.0 to the network interface eth0.

- Checking Network Connectivity: You can use the ping command to check if a device with a specific IP address is reachable on the network.

Exercises:

1. Determine the subnet mask for the following CIDR notations:
    - 192.168.1.0/28
    - 10.0.0.0/16
    - 172.16.0.0/20
2. Write a Bash script that takes an IP address and subnet mask as arguments and calculates the network address.
3. Research the ipcalc command and learn how to use it to perform IP address calculations and subnetting.

Understanding IP addresses and subnetting is fundamental to working with networks. By mastering these concepts, you'll be able to write Bash scripts that effectively configure network devices and control network traffic.

2.3 Network Protocols

A network protocol is a set of rules or procedures that govern the format and transmission of data between two or more devices on a network.[2] It defines how data is packaged, addressed, transmitted, received, and interpreted.

Just like different types of vehicles (cars, trucks, motorcycles) follow different rules, different types of network traffic use different protocols. Some protocols prioritize reliability, while others prioritize speed.[3] Some protocols are used for specific applications, like email or web browsing.[4]

TCP/IP (Transmission Control Protocol/Internet Protocol)

TCP/IP is the foundational protocol suite of the internet.[5] It's a combination of two essential protocols:

- TCP (Transmission Control Protocol): TCP is like a reliable courier service.[6] It ensures that data is delivered reliably and in order.[7] It does this by:
    - Establishing a connection between the sender and receiver before transmitting data.[8]
    - Breaking data into smaller packets and numbering them.[9]
    - Checking for errors and retransmitting lost packets.[10]
    - Ensuring that packets are delivered in the correct order.[11]
- IP (Internet Protocol): IP is like the postal service.[12] It handles the addressing and routing of data packets. It's responsible for:
    - Assigning unique IP addresses to devices.[13]
    - Encapsulating data into packets.[14]

- Routing packets across different networks to reach their destination.[15]

TCP/IP is a robust and reliable protocol suite, making it ideal for applications that require guaranteed delivery of data, such as web browsing, email, and file transfer.[16]

UDP (User Datagram Protocol)

UDP is a connectionless protocol, which means it doesn't establish a connection before transmitting data.[17] It's like sending a letter without a tracking number – you don't know for sure if it will arrive, or in what order it will arrive compared to other letters.

UDP is faster and more efficient than TCP because it doesn't have the overhead of connection establishment and error checking.[18] However, it doesn't guarantee delivery or order of data.

UDP is suitable for applications where speed is more important than reliability, such as streaming video, online games, and DNS lookups.[19]

ICMP (Internet Control Message Protocol)

ICMP is a network protocol used for network diagnostics and error reporting.[20] It's like the traffic control system that monitors road conditions and alerts drivers of accidents or congestion.

ICMP is used by tools like ping and traceroute to:

- Check network connectivity: ping sends ICMP echo requests to a target device and waits for ICMP echo replies. If replies are received, it indicates that the device is reachable.
- Diagnose network problems: traceroute sends a series of ICMP packets with increasing Time-to-Live (TTL) values. This allows it to trace the path of the packets through the network and identify any routers or links that are causing delays or dropping packets.[21]

Understanding these network protocols is crucial for writing Bash scripts that interact with network services and diagnose network problems. You'll often use commands that rely on these protocols:

- ping: Uses ICMP to check network connectivity.[22]
- traceroute: Uses ICMP to trace the route to a remote host.[23]
- tcpdump: Captures and analyzes TCP/IP packets.[24]
- nc **(netcat):** A versatile tool that can use both TCP and UDP for various network tasks.[25]

Real-World Examples:

- Monitoring Network Performance: You can use ping in a Bash script to continuously monitor the availability of a critical server and send an alert if it becomes unreachable.
- Troubleshooting Network Issues: You can use traceroute in a script to identify network bottlenecks or connectivity problems.
- Analyzing Network Traffic: You can use tcpdump to capture network traffic and analyze it for suspicious activity or performance issues.

Exercises:

1. Write a Bash script that pings a list of servers and reports which ones are reachable and which ones are not.
2. Write a Bash script that uses traceroute to trace the route to a remote server and saves the output to a file.
3. Research the nc command and learn how to use it to test network connectivity using both TCP and UDP.

2.4 Network Services

A network service is an application that runs on a server and listens for requests from clients. When a client sends a request, the server processes the request and sends back a response. This communication typically happens over a specific port using a defined protocol.

For example, when you browse the web, your web browser (the client) sends requests to a web server (like Apache or Nginx) using the HTTP protocol over port 80. The web server then sends back the requested web page as a response.

Common Network Services:

Here are some of the most common network services you'll encounter:

- HTTP (Hypertext Transfer Protocol): This is the foundation of the World Wide Web. It's the protocol used by web browsers and web servers to communicate and exchange web pages and other content. HTTP is a stateless protocol, meaning each request is treated independently.
    - HTTPS (HTTP Secure): This is a secure version of HTTP that encrypts communication between the client and server, protecting sensitive information like passwords and credit card numbers.
- SSH (Secure Shell): This is a cryptographic network protocol that provides a secure way to access and manage a remote computer. It's commonly used by system administrators to log in to servers, execute commands, and transfer files. SSH provides strong authentication and encryption, making it much more secure than older protocols like Telnet.
- FTP (File Transfer Protocol): This is a standard network protocol used to transfer files between a client and a server on a computer network. You can use FTP to upload files to a web server, download files from a remote computer, or transfer files between two servers.
    - SFTP (Secure File Transfer Protocol): This is a secure version of FTP that encrypts data during transfer, providing confidentiality and integrity.
- DNS (Domain Name System): This is a hierarchical and decentralized naming system for computers, services, or

other resources connected to the internet[1] or a private network. It translates human-readable domain names (like www.google.com) into numerical IP addresses, allowing users to access websites and services without having to remember IP addresses.

Bash scripting provides powerful tools to interact with these network services. You can use commands and utilities to automate tasks related to these services.

Real-World Examples:

- Automating Website Backups: You can use wget (a command-line utility that retrieves content from web servers) in a Bash script to download website files regularly and create backups.
- Managing Remote Servers: You can use ssh in a Bash script to connect to remote servers, execute commands, and automate system administration tasks.
- Transferring Files: You can use scp (secure copy) or sftp in a Bash script to securely transfer files between servers or to upload files to a web server.
- Checking DNS Records: You can use dig or nslookup in a Bash script to query DNS servers and retrieve information about domain names, IP addresses, and other DNS records.

Exercises:

1. Write a Bash script that uses wget to download a specific web page and save it to a file.
2. Write a Bash script that uses ssh to connect to a remote server and execute a command (e.g., ls -l).
3. Write a Bash script that uses scp to copy a file from your local machine to a remote server.
4. Write a Bash script that uses dig to retrieve the IP address of a given domain name.

2.5 Network Topologies and Architectures

Network topology refers to the arrangement of the various elements (links, nodes, etc.) of a computer network. Essentially, it's a map of how devices are connected. There are several common network topologies, each with its own advantages and disadvantages:

- Bus Topology: In a bus topology, all devices are connected to a single cable, often referred to as the "bus" or "backbone." This is a simple and inexpensive topology, but it has some limitations. If the main cable fails, the entire network goes down. Also, as more devices are added, the network can become slow due to data collisions.
- Star Topology: In a star topology, all devices are connected to a central hub or switch. This is a more robust topology because a failure in one device doesn't affect the others. It also offers better performance than a bus topology, as the central hub manages data traffic more efficiently. Most home and small office networks use a star topology.
- Ring Topology: In a ring topology, devices are connected in a closed loop or ring. Data travels around the ring in one direction, and each device acts as a repeater, passing the data along to the next device. This topology can be efficient for small networks, but a failure in any one device can disrupt the entire network.
- Mesh Topology: In a mesh topology, devices are interconnected with multiple paths. This provides redundancy and fault tolerance, as data can take alternative routes if one link fails. Mesh topologies are often used in critical networks where high availability is essential, such as in telecommunications or industrial control systems. There are two types of mesh topologies:
    - Full Mesh: Every device is connected directly to every other device.

- Partial Mesh: Some devices are connected to all other devices, while others are only connected to those they exchange data with most frequently.

- Tree Topology: This topology combines characteristics of the bus and star topologies. It has a hierarchical structure with a root node at the top and branches extending downwards. This topology is often used in large networks where devices are grouped into departments or organizational units.

- Hybrid Topology: A hybrid topology combines two or more different topologies. This is common in large networks that need to accommodate different requirements and geographical locations.

Network Architectures

Network architecture refers to the overall design and structure of a network, including the hardware, software, and protocols used. It defines how the network is organized and how different components interact.

Here are some key aspects of network architecture:

- Layered Architecture: Networks are often designed using a layered approach, such as the OSI model or the TCP/IP model. This helps to break down complex network functions into manageable layers, making it easier to design, implement, and troubleshoot.

- Client-Server Architecture: This is a common architecture where clients (e.g., computers, smartphones) request services from servers (e.g., web servers, file servers). The servers provide resources and functionality to the clients.

- Peer-to-Peer Architecture: In this architecture, all devices on the network can act as both clients and servers, sharing resources directly with each other.

- Cloud Computing Architecture: This involves using remote servers hosted on the internet to store and process data, rather than relying on local servers. Cloud computing offers scalability, flexibility, and cost-effectiveness.

Understanding network topologies and architectures can help you:

- Write scripts that are tailored to your network environment: For example, if you're working with a star topology, you might write scripts to monitor the central switch or manage connections to individual devices.
- Troubleshoot network problems more effectively: Knowing the topology can help you identify potential points of failure or bottlenecks.
- Design and implement network automation solutions: You can use Bash scripts to automate tasks like network configuration, monitoring, and security management, taking into account the specific topology and architecture of your network.

Real-World Examples:

- Monitoring a network with a star topology: You could write a Bash script that uses ping to monitor the availability of all devices connected to the central switch.
- Managing a network with a tree topology: You could write scripts to automate software updates or configuration changes for devices in specific branches of the network.
- Automating tasks in a cloud environment: You could write Bash scripts to manage virtual machines, configure network settings, or monitor cloud resources.

Exercises:

1. Draw a diagram of your home network topology. Identify the devices and how they are connected.
2. Research different cloud computing architectures (e.g., AWS, Azure, GCP) and their key components.

3. Think about how you could use Bash scripts to automate tasks in your network environment, taking into account its topology and architecture.

By understanding network topologies and architectures, you gain a holistic view of how networks are structured and organized. This knowledge will help you write more effective Bash scripts for network management, troubleshooting, and automation.

Chapter 3: Bash Networking Tools

Now that you have a solid grasp of networking fundamentals, let's discuss the powerful tools that Bash provides for interacting with and managing networks. These tools are like your network command center, giving you the ability to monitor, configure, and troubleshoot your network infrastructure right from your terminal.

3.1 Core Network Utilities

Let's explore some of the most fundamental network utilities available in Bash. These are the tools you'll use day in and day out to gather information about your network, diagnose connectivity problems, and troubleshoot DNS issues. Think of them as your essential toolkit for network exploration and troubleshooting.

ping (Packet Internet Groper)[1]

ping is your go-to command for checking the basic connectivity between your machine and another device on the network. It works by sending ICMP (Internet Control Message Protocol) echo requests to the target device and waiting for ICMP echo replies.[2]

Here's the basic syntax:

```
Bash
```

```
ping [options] <destination>
```

- <destination> can be an IP address or a domain name.

Here are some commonly used options:

- -c <count>: Specifies the number of echo requests to send.
- -i <interval>: Specifies the time interval between requests (in seconds).

- -W <timeout>: Specifies the timeout in seconds before ping gives up waiting for a reply.

Example:

Bash

```
ping -c 4 www.google.com
```

This will send 4 ICMP echo requests to www.google.com and display the results, including the round-trip time (RTT), packet loss, and statistics.

How ping **Helps:**

- Testing Connectivity: ping quickly tells you if a device is reachable on the network.
- Measuring Latency: The RTT values provide an indication of the network delay between your machine and the target.[3]
- Identifying Packet Loss: If any packets are lost, it might indicate network congestion or problems along the route.[4]

traceroute

traceroute is used to trace the route that packets take to reach a destination host. It helps you identify the intermediate routers or hops involved in the path.

Bash

```
traceroute www.example.com
```

This command sends a series of UDP packets with increasing Time-to-Live (TTL) values. Each router along the path decrements the TTL by one.[5] When the TTL reaches zero, the router sends an ICMP "Time Exceeded" message back to the source.[6] By analyzing these messages, traceroute can map out the network path.

How traceroute **Helps:**

- Diagnosing Network Problems: traceroute can help you pinpoint where network delays or connectivity issues are occurring. If you see a large increase in latency or packet loss at a particular hop, it might indicate a problem with that router or link.
- Understanding Network Topology: traceroute provides a visual representation of the network path, giving you insights into the network's structure.

nslookup

nslookup is a command-line tool used for querying DNS (Domain Name System) servers. It allows you to look up the IP address associated with a domain name or vice versa.

Bash

```
nslookup www.facebook.com
```

This will query the default DNS server to find the IP address of www.facebook.com.

You can also use nslookup to perform reverse DNS lookups (finding the domain name associated with an IP address) and to query specific DNS records (like MX records for mail servers).

dig (Domain Information Groper)[7]

dig is another DNS lookup tool that is more flexible and provides more detailed information than nslookup.

Bash

```
dig www.amazon.com
```

This will query the DNS server for information about www.amazon.com, including its IP address, name servers, and other DNS records.

dig offers many options for customizing queries, specifying DNS servers, and retrieving specific types of records.

whois

whois is used to retrieve information about a domain name or IP address. This information typically includes:

- Domain registrar
- Registration date
- Expiration date
- Contact information (administrative, technical)
- Name servers

Bash

```
whois google.com
```

This will display registration information about google.com.

Real-World Examples:

- Troubleshooting Website Access: If you can't access a website, you can use ping to check if the web server is reachable. If the ping fails, you can use traceroute to see where the connection is failing. You can also use nslookup or dig to check if the domain name is resolving correctly to an IP address.
- Monitoring Network Performance: You can use ping in a Bash script to continuously monitor the latency to a critical server and send an alert if the latency exceeds a certain threshold.

- Investigating Network Security Incidents: You can use whois to gather information about suspicious domain names or IP addresses.

Exercises:

1. Use ping to test the connectivity to different websites and compare the RTT values.
2. Use traceroute to trace the route to a website hosted in another country. Observe the different hops and their locations.
3. Use nslookup and dig to query different types of DNS records (A, MX, NS, CNAME) for a domain name.
4. Use whois to look up information about your own domain name or a website you frequently visit.

By mastering these core network utilities, you'll have a solid foundation for diagnosing network problems, gathering network information, and automating network tasks with Bash scripts.

3.2 Interface and Connection Management

Let's discuss the essential tools Bash provides for managing network interfaces and connections. These tools allow you to view and configure network settings, monitor active connections, and gather valuable information about your network's status.[1] Think of them as your dashboard for understanding and controlling the flow of data in and out of your system.

ifconfig

ifconfig (interface configuration) is a classic command-line utility used to display and configure network interface parameters. It's been around for a long time and is available on most Unix-like systems.[2]

Viewing Interface Information:

Bash

```
ifconfig
```

This command displays information about all active network interfaces on your system. You'll see details like:

- Interface Name: (e.g., etho, wlano, lo)
- Hardware Address (MAC address): The unique physical address of the interface.[3]
- IP Address: The IP address assigned to the interface.[4]
- Subnet Mask: The subnet mask associated with the IP address.[5]
- RX and TX statistics: Information about received and transmitted data (packets, errors, dropped packets).

To view information about a specific interface, you can specify the interface name:

Bash

```
ifconfig eth0
```

Configuring Interfaces (with caution):

ifconfig can also be used to configure network interfaces, such as assigning IP addresses, setting up network masks, and bringing interfaces up or down. However, it's important to note that ifconfig is being gradually deprecated in favor of the more modern ip command. For most configuration tasks, it's recommended to use **ip.**

ip

ip is a powerful and versatile command-line tool for managing network interfaces, routing tables, and other network configuration aspects. It's part of the iproute2 package and is considered the modern replacement for ifconfig.

Viewing Interface Information:

Bash

```
ip addr show
```

This command displays information about all network interfaces, similar to ifconfig. You can also use ip link show to view interface status and link information.

Configuring Interfaces:

Bash

```
sudo ip addr add 192.168.1.10/24 dev eth0   # Add
an IP address

sudo ip link set eth0 up                    # Bring
the interface up

sudo ip link set eth0 down                  # Bring
the interface down
```

ip provides a wide range of subcommands for managing different aspects of network configuration.

netstat

netstat (network statistics) is a command-line tool used to display network connections, routing tables, interface statistics, masquerade connections, and multicast memberships.[6]

Viewing Active Connections:

```
Bash
```

```
netstat -an
```

This displays all active network connections, including the protocol (TCP, UDP), local address, foreign address, and state.

Other Useful Options:

- -t: Show TCP connections.
- -u: Show UDP connections.
- -l: Show listening sockets (servers).
- -p: Show the process ID and name associated with each socket.

ss (Socket Statistics)

ss is a modern replacement for netstat. It provides similar information but is considered more efficient and reliable.

```
Bash
```

```
ss -tulpn
```

This displays listening TCP and UDP sockets, including the process ID and program name associated with each socket.

Real-World Examples:

- Troubleshooting Network Connectivity: If you're experiencing network issues, you can use ifconfig or ip addr show to check the status of your network interface, its IP address, and whether it's properly configured. You can also use netstat or ss to see if there are any active connections or listening services that might be causing problems.
- Monitoring Network Traffic: You can use netstat or ss to monitor active network connections and identify any unusual activity. You can also use these tools to track the number of connections to a particular service or port.

- Dynamically Configuring Network Interfaces: You can use ip in Bash scripts to dynamically configure network interfaces, such as assigning IP addresses based on certain conditions or changing network settings in response to network events.

Exercises:

1. Use ifconfig and ip addr show to compare the information they display about your network interfaces.
2. Use ip to configure a static IP address on a network interface.
3. Use netstat and ss to view active network connections and identify the processes associated with them.
4. Write a Bash script that uses ip to bring a network interface up or down based on a command-line argument.

3.3 Network Packet Analysis

Network packet analysis involves capturing network traffic and examining the contents of individual packets. These packets are like envelopes carrying data between devices on the network. By opening these envelopes and inspecting the data, you can understand what's happening on your network at a very granular level.

tcpdump

tcpdump is a powerful command-line tool that allows you to capture and analyze network packets. It's like a network microscope, letting you zoom in on the details of network communication.

Capturing Packets:

The basic syntax for capturing packets is:

```Bash
tcpdump [options]
```

This will capture all packets on the default network interface. Here are some commonly used options:

- -i <interface>: Specifies the network interface to capture on (e.g., eth0, wlan0).
- -w <filename>: Writes the captured packets to a file (in pcap format).
- -r <filename>: Reads packets from a previously captured file.
- -n: Don't resolve hostnames or port numbers.
- -v: Verbose output (more details).
- -vv: Even more verbose output.

Filtering Packets:

tcpdump provides a rich filtering language that allows you to capture only the packets you're interested in. Here are some examples:

- tcpdump -i eth0 host 192.168.1.10: Capture packets to or from host 192.168.1.10.
- tcpdump -i eth0 port 80: Capture packets on port 80 (HTTP traffic).
- tcpdump -i eth0 src host 192.168.1.10 and dst port 22: Capture SSH traffic from host 192.168.1.10.
- tcpdump -i eth0 tcp and not port 22: Capture all TCP traffic except SSH.

Analyzing Packets:

tcpdump displays the captured packets in a human-readable format, showing information like:

- Timestamp

- Source and destination IP addresses and ports
- Protocol (TCP, UDP, ICMP, etc.)
- Packet length
- Packet contents (in hexadecimal and ASCII)

Wireshark

Wireshark is a popular graphical network protocol analyzer. It provides a user-friendly interface for capturing, filtering, and analyzing network traffic.

Key Features:

- Packet Capture: Wireshark can capture packets from live network interfaces or read packets from captured files.
- Packet Filtering: Wireshark provides a powerful filtering system to isolate specific packets based on various criteria.
- Packet Inspection: Wireshark displays the contents of packets in a hierarchical format, allowing you to drill down into the details of each protocol layer.
- Protocol Decoding: Wireshark supports a wide range of protocols and can decode the contents of packets to provide meaningful information.
- Statistics and Graphs: Wireshark provides various statistics and graphs to help you visualize network traffic patterns and identify anomalies.

tshark (Command-line Wireshark)

Wireshark also provides a command-line version called tshark, which offers similar functionality to tcpdump but with more advanced filtering and analysis capabilities.

Real-World Examples:

- Troubleshooting Network Performance: You can use tcpdump or Wireshark to capture network traffic and analyze it for performance bottlenecks, such as high latency or packet loss.

- Identifying Network Security Threats: You can use these tools to detect suspicious network activity, such as port scans, denial-of-service attacks, or malware communication.
- Debugging Application Issues: You can capture traffic between an application and a server to diagnose communication problems or identify performance issues.
- Analyzing Network Protocols: You can use Wireshark to study the details of network protocols and understand how they work.

Exercises:

1. Use tcpdump to capture traffic on your network interface and filter it to display only HTTP traffic.
2. Use Wireshark to capture traffic and analyze a specific TCP conversation between your computer and a web server.
3. Use tshark to capture packets and filter them based on specific criteria (e.g., source IP address, destination port, protocol).
4. Research common network attacks and learn how to use tcpdump or Wireshark to detect them.

3.4 Network Scanning

Network scanning is the process of identifying active hosts on a network and discovering information about them. It's like taking inventory of all the devices connected to your network and understanding what services they are running. This information is crucial for network management, security auditing, and troubleshooting.

nmap Basics

nmap is a command-line tool that provides a wide range of scanning techniques and options. The basic syntax is:

Bash

```
nmap [options] <target>
```

- <target> can be a single IP address, a hostname, a range of IP addresses, or a network in CIDR notation (e.g., 192.168.1.0/24).

Basic Scanning Techniques:

- TCP Connect Scan (-sT): This is the most basic scan type. It establishes a full TCP connection to each port on the target. It's reliable but can be easily detected.
- TCP SYN Scan (-sS): This is a stealthier scan type. It sends a SYN packet to each port and checks for a SYN/ACK response. It doesn't complete the TCP handshake, making it less detectable.
- UDP Scan (-sU): This scan type sends UDP packets to each port and checks for a response. UDP scans can be slower and less reliable than TCP scans because UDP is a connectionless protocol.
- Ping Scan (-sP): This scan type sends ICMP echo requests (like ping) to discover active hosts on a network.

Example:

Bash

```
nmap -sS 192.168.1.0/24
```

This will perform a TCP SYN scan of the network 192.168.1.0/24, identifying active hosts and open ports.

Advanced Scanning Options:

- OS Detection (-O): nmap can attempt to determine the operating system of the target host by analyzing its network responses.
- Version Detection (-sV): nmap can try to identify the versions of services running on the target host (e.g., web server version, SSH version).
- Script Scanning (-sC): nmap can run scripts to gather additional information about the target, such as vulnerabilities, web server configuration, and more.
- Firewall/IDS Evasion (-f, -D): nmap provides options to try to evade firewalls and intrusion detection systems.

Example:

```Bash
nmap -A 192.168.1.10
```

This will perform a comprehensive scan of the host 192.168.1.10, including OS detection, version detection, script scanning, and traceroute.

Output and Interpretation:

nmap provides detailed output about the scan results, including:

- Host status (up or down)
- Open ports and services
- OS and version information
- Script scan results

It's important to understand how to interpret this output to identify potential security vulnerabilities or network misconfigurations.

Real-World Examples:

- **Network Inventory:** You can use nmap to discover all devices on your network and create an inventory of active hosts.
- **Security Auditing:** You can use nmap to identify open ports, running services, and potential vulnerabilities on your systems.
- **Penetration Testing:** Security professionals use nmap as a key tool for penetration testing to identify weaknesses in network security.
- **Troubleshooting Network Connectivity:** You can use nmap to check if specific ports are open on a remote server or to identify firewall rules that might be blocking traffic.

Exercises:

1. Perform a basic scan of your home network using nmap. Identify the active hosts and their open ports.
2. Use nmap with OS detection to identify the operating systems of devices on your network.
3. Use nmap with version detection to identify the versions of services running on a web server.
4. Research nmap scripting engine (NSE) and learn how to use scripts to gather more information about your network.

Chapter 4: Network Interface Configuration

We've discussed the essential networking concepts and tools, let's go into the practical application of Bash scripting for automating network interface configuration. This is where you'll learn how to use Bash to manage IP addresses, control network interfaces, and configure virtual LANs (VLANs), all from the command line.

4.1 Dynamic IP Configuration

Dynamic IP configuration with Bash is a crucial skill for managing networks in today's world, where IP addresses can change frequently. Think of it like navigating a city where street names change every day – you need a way to find your destination even if the address isn't fixed.

Why Dynamic IP Configuration?

Dynamic IP configuration is essential in several scenarios:

- DHCP (Dynamic Host Configuration Protocol): DHCP is a network protocol that automates the process of assigning IP addresses to devices on a network. Most home and small office networks, as well as many larger networks, use DHCP to simplify network administration.
- Cloud Environments: Cloud providers like AWS, Azure, and GCP often use dynamic IP addresses for virtual machines. This allows them to manage IP address allocation efficiently and scale their infrastructure easily.
- Mobile Devices: Laptops, smartphones, and tablets that connect to different Wi-Fi networks need to obtain new IP addresses each time they join a new network.

Understanding DHCP

DHCP works on a client-server model. When a device (the client) connects to a network, it sends a DHCP request to a DHCP server (usually a router). The server responds with an IP address, subnet mask, default gateway, and other network configuration parameters. The client then uses this information to configure its network interface.

dhclient - Your DHCP Client

In Linux, the dhclient command is a DHCP client that allows you to interact with DHCP servers. You can use it to request an IP address, renew an existing lease, or release an IP address.

Requesting an IP Address:

Bash

```
sudo dhclient eth0
```

This command sends a DHCP request on the interface etho and obtains an IP address and other network configuration parameters from the DHCP server.

Renewing a Lease:

Bash

```
sudo dhclient -r eth0   # Release the current IP
address

sudo dhclient eth0      # Request a new IP address
(often the same one)
```

This renews the DHCP lease, ensuring that you continue to have a valid IP address.

Releasing an IP Address:

Bash

```bash
sudo dhclient -r eth0
```

This releases the IP address back to the DHCP server, making it available for other devices.

Scripting Dynamic IP Configuration with Bash

Now, let's see how you can use Bash scripting to automate dynamic IP configuration. You can incorporate dhclient into your scripts to manage IP addresses efficiently.

Example: Checking and Requesting an IP Address

Bash

```bash
#!/bin/bash

interface="eth0"

# Check if the interface has an IP address

ip_address=$(ip addr show dev $interface | grep
"inet " | awk '{print $2}')

if [ -z "$ip_address" ]; then

   echo "No IP address found on $interface.
Requesting DHCP..."

   sudo dhclient $interface

else

   echo "IP address on $interface: $ip_address"

fi
```

This script checks if the specified interface has an IP address. If not, it uses dhclient to request one.

Example: Periodically Renewing an IP Address

Bash

```bash
#!/bin/bash

interface="wlan0"

while true; do

  echo "Renewing IP address on $interface..."

  sudo dhclient -r $interface

  sudo dhclient $interface

  sleep 3600  # Sleep for 1 hour

done
```

This script runs in a loop and renews the IP address on the wlan0 interface every hour.

Real-World Examples:

- Cloud Instances: You can use Bash scripts with dhclient to ensure that your cloud instances always have a valid IP address, even if the provider changes it dynamically.
- Network Monitoring: You can write scripts to monitor the IP addresses of critical devices and send alerts if they change unexpectedly.
- Automated Network Configuration: You can create scripts that automatically configure network interfaces with dynamic IP addresses during system startup or after network changes.

Exercises:

1. Write a Bash script that checks if a specific interface has a valid IP address and, if not, requests a new one using dhclient.
2. Modify the script to also display the subnet mask and default gateway obtained from the DHCP server.
3. Write a Bash script that releases the IP address of an interface when the system shuts down.

By mastering dynamic IP configuration with Bash, you can manage network interfaces efficiently in environments where IP addresses change frequently. This is a valuable skill for any network administrator or engineer working with modern networks.

4.2 Managing Network Interfaces

Let's discuss how to manage network interfaces with Bash. This is like having the control panel for your network connections right at your fingertips. You can use Bash commands to bring interfaces up or down, configure their settings, and monitor their status. This gives you fine-grained control over how your system interacts with the network.

Why Manage Network Interfaces?

Managing network interfaces is essential for several reasons:

- Troubleshooting Network Issues: If you're experiencing connectivity problems, you might need to restart an interface, change its settings, or check its status to diagnose the issue.[1]
- Security: You might need to disable an interface temporarily to prevent unauthorized access or isolate a part of your network.

- Dynamic Network Configuration: You might need to change network settings in response to changing network conditions or to automate network configuration tasks.
- Virtualization: If you're working with virtual machines, you'll need to manage the virtual network interfaces to ensure proper communication between the host and the guests.

The ip Command

The ip command is your primary tool for managing network interfaces in Linux. It's a powerful and versatile command that provides a wide range of subcommands for configuring various aspects of networking.[2]

Bringing Interfaces Up or Down

To bring an interface up (enable it):

Bash

```
sudo ip link set eth0 up
```

To bring an interface down (disable it):

Bash

```
sudo ip link set eth0 dow
```

Displaying Interface Status

To view the status of an interface:

Bash

```
ip link show eth0
```

This will show you whether the interface is up or down, its MAC address, MTU (Maximum Transmission Unit), and other information.

You can also use the ethtool command to get more detailed information about an interface, including its speed, duplex mode, and link status:

Bash

```
ethtool eth0
```

Configuring IP Addresses

To assign an IP address to an interface:

Bash

```
sudo ip addr add 192.168.1.10/24 dev eth0
```

To remove an IP address from an interface:

Bash

```
sudo ip addr del 192.168.1.10/24 dev eth0
```

Configuring Other Interface Parameters

You can use ip to configure other interface parameters, such as:

- MTU (Maximum Transmission Unit): The maximum size of a packet that can be transmitted on the interface.[3]
- Promiscuous Mode: Allows the interface to capture all network traffic, even if it's not addressed to it.[4] This is useful for network monitoring and analysis.

Scripting Interface Management with Bash

You can incorporate these ip commands into your Bash scripts to automate interface management tasks.

Example: Checking and Bringing Up an Interface

Bash

```
#!/bin/bash

interface="eth0"

# Check if the interface is up

if ip link show dev $interface | grep -q "state UP"; then

  echo "$interface is already up."

else

  echo "$interface is down. Bringing it up..."

  sudo ip link set dev $interface up

fi
```

This script checks if the specified interface is up. If not, it brings it up.

Example: Configuring an Interface with Dynamic IP

Bash

```
#!/bin/bash

interface="wlan0"

# Bring the interface up

sudo ip link set dev $interface up

# Request an IP address using DHCP
```

```
sudo dhclient $interface

# Display the assigned IP address

ip_address=$(ip addr show dev $interface | grep
"inet " | awk '{print $2}')

echo "IP address on $interface: $ip_address"
```

This script brings up a wireless interface and then uses dhclient to obtain a dynamic IP address.

Real-World Examples:

- Automated Network Failover: You can write a Bash script that monitors the status of a primary network interface and automatically switches to a backup interface if the primary one fails.
- Network Configuration Management: You can use Bash scripts to manage network configurations across multiple servers, ensuring consistency and reducing manual effort.[5]
- Dynamic Network Adaptation: You can write scripts that adjust network interface settings in response to changing network conditions, such as bandwidth availability or security threats.

Exercises:

1. Write a Bash script that takes an interface name as an argument and displays its status (up or down), MAC address, and IP address.
2. Write a Bash script that brings down all network interfaces except for the loopback interface (lo).
3. Write a Bash script that changes the MTU of an interface.
4. Research the tc (traffic control) command and learn how to use it with Bash scripts to manage network traffic shaping and quality of service (QoS).

4.3 Configuring VLANs

VLANs (Virtual LANs) are a powerful tool for network segmentation, allowing you to divide a physical network into multiple logical networks. Think of it like partitioning a large office building into separate departments or workspaces. Each VLAN acts as its own isolated network, even though they share the same physical infrastructure.

Why Use VLANs?

VLANs offer several benefits:

- Improved Security: By isolating different departments or user groups into separate VLANs, you can limit the impact of security breaches and control access to sensitive resources.
- Enhanced Performance: VLANs reduce network congestion by limiting broadcast traffic to a specific VLAN, improving overall network performance.
- Simplified Management: VLANs make it easier to manage and organize network resources by grouping devices with similar needs or functions.
- Flexibility: VLANs provide flexibility in network design, allowing you to easily move devices between VLANs without physical reconfiguration.

A VLAN is a logical grouping of devices on a network that behave as if they are on their own separate network, regardless of their physical location. Devices within a VLAN can communicate with each other as if they were on a dedicated network segment, even if they are physically connected to different switches.

Each VLAN is identified by a VLAN ID (VID), which is a number between 1 and 4094. Devices are assigned to a VLAN either through port-based VLANs (configuring the switch port) or through MAC-based VLANs (based on the device's MAC address).

Configuring VLANs with ip

The ip command provides the necessary tools to create and manage VLAN interfaces in Linux.

Creating a VLAN Interface:

Bash

```
sudo ip link add link eth0 name eth0.10 type vlan
id 10
```

This command creates a VLAN interface named eth0.10 on the physical interface eth0 with VLAN ID 10.

Assigning an IP Address:

Once you've created the VLAN interface, you can assign an IP address to it just like you would with a physical interface:

Bash

```
sudo ip addr add 192.168.10.10/24 dev eth0.10
```

Bringing the Interface Up:

Bash

```
sudo ip link set eth0.10 up
```

This activates the VLAN interface, allowing it to communicate with other devices on the same VLAN.

Deleting a VLAN Interface:

```bash
Bash

sudo ip link delete eth0.10
```

Listing VLAN Interfaces:

You can list all VLAN interfaces on a system using:

```bash
Bash

ip -d link show type vlan
```

Scripting VLAN Configuration with Bash

You can use these ip commands in your Bash scripts to automate VLAN configuration.

Example: Creating a VLAN Interface

```bash
Bash

#!/bin/bash

physical_interface="eth0"

vlan_id="10"

vlan_interface="$physical_interface.$vlan_id"

ip_address="192.168.10.10/24"

# Create the VLAN interface

sudo ip link add link $physical_interface name
$vlan_interface type vlan id $vlan_id

# Assign an IP address
```

```
sudo ip addr add $ip_address dev $vlan_interface

# Bring the interface up

sudo ip link set dev $vlan_interface up

echo "VLAN interface $vlan_interface created with
IP address $ip_address"
```

This script creates a VLAN interface with the specified VLAN ID and IP address.

Real-World Examples:

- Network Segmentation in a Company: You can use VLANs to separate departments (e.g., marketing, finance, IT) into different logical networks, improving security and performance.
- Guest Wi-Fi Networks: You can create a separate VLAN for guest Wi-Fi access, isolating guest traffic from your internal network.
- IoT Devices: You can create a dedicated VLAN for IoT devices, preventing them from accessing critical systems on your network.

Exercises:

1. Create a VLAN interface on your system with a specific VLAN ID and assign an IP address to it.
2. Write a Bash script that creates multiple VLAN interfaces on a physical interface, each with its own VLAN ID and IP address.
3. Research how to configure VLANs on your router or switch and experiment with different VLAN configurations.

4.4 Wireless Network Configuration

To configure wireless networks using Bash is essential for managing laptops, smartphones, and other devices that connect to Wi-Fi networks. Think of it like having a universal remote control for all your wireless connections, allowing you to scan for networks, connect to them securely, and even automate the process.

Wireless networks use radio waves to transmit data between devices.[1] A wireless network typically consists of:

- **Wireless Access Point (WAP):** This is the central device that provides wireless connectivity, often a router with Wi-Fi capabilities.[2]
- **Wireless Clients:** These are the devices that connect to the WAP, such as laptops, smartphones, and tablets.[3]
- **ESSID (Extended Service Set Identifier):** This is the name of the wireless network (e.g., "MyHomeWiFi").[4]
- **Security Protocols:** Wireless networks use security protocols like WPA (Wi-Fi Protected Access) or WPA2 to encrypt data and prevent unauthorized access.[5]

Wireless Tools in Bash

Bash provides several command-line tools for managing wireless networks:

- iwconfig**:** This command is used to display and configure wireless interface parameters.[6]

Bash

```
iwconfig wlan0
```

This will display information about the wireless interface wlan0, including the ESSID (network name), signal strength, and encryption settings.

- iwlist: This command is used to scan for available wireless networks and display their information.[7]

Bash

```
iwlist wlan0 scan
```

This will scan for wireless networks in range and display their ESSIDs, signal strengths, security modes, and other details.

- wpa_supplicant: This is a Wi-Fi client that allows you to connect to wireless networks and manage security settings.[8] It's commonly used to connect to WPA/WPA2-protected networks.

Connecting to a Wireless Network

To connect to a wireless network using wpa_supplicant, you typically need to create a configuration file (wpa_supplicant.conf) with the network credentials (ESSID and password).

Example wpa_supplicant.conf **file:**

```
ctrl_interface=/var/run/wpa_supplicant

network={

    ssid="MyHomeWiFi"

    psk="mysecretpassword"

}
```

Then, you can use the wpa_supplicant command to connect to the network:

Bash

```
sudo     wpa_supplicant     -i     wlan0     -c
wpa_supplicant.conf
```

This will initiate the connection process to the network specified in the configuration file.

Obtaining an IP Address:

Once connected, you can use dhclient to obtain an IP address from the network's DHCP server:

Bash

```
sudo dhclient wlan0
```

Scripting Wireless Configuration with Bash

You can use these tools in your Bash scripts to automate wireless network configuration.

Example: Connecting to a Network

Bash

```
#!/bin/bash

interface="wlan0"

ssid="MyHomeWiFi"

password="mysecretpassword"

# Create a temporary wpa_supplicant configuration file

wpa_config=$(mktemp)

cat << EOF > $wpa_config

ctrl_interface=/var/run/wpa_supplicant
```

```
network={

    ssid="$ssid"

    psk="$password"

}

EOF

# Connect to the network

sudo wpa_supplicant -i $interface -c $wpa_config

# Obtain an IP address

sudo dhclient $interface

# Remove the temporary configuration file

rm $wpa_config

echo "Connected to network $ssid"
```

This script creates a temporary configuration file, connects to the specified network using wpa_supplicant, obtains an IP address, and then removes the temporary file.

Real-World Examples:

- Automated Wi-Fi Connection: You can create a script that automatically connects your laptop to your home Wi-Fi network when you arrive home.
- Managing Multiple Wireless Networks: You can write a script that allows you to easily switch between different Wi-Fi networks based on your location or needs.
- Wireless Network Monitoring: You can use Bash scripts to monitor the signal strength and quality of your wireless connection and send alerts if there are problems.

Exercises:

1. Use iwlist to scan for available wireless networks and display their information.
2. Create a wpa_supplicant.conf file and use it to connect to a WPA/WPA2-protected network.
3. Write a Bash script that automatically connects to a wireless network and obtains an IP address.
4. Research the iw command, a newer and more powerful tool for managing wireless interfaces, and explore its capabilities.

By mastering wireless network configuration with Bash, you can manage your wireless connections more efficiently and automate tasks related to connecting to and managing Wi-Fi networks. This is a valuable skill for anyone who works with wireless devices and needs to ensure seamless connectivity in various environments.

Chapter 5: Managing Routing and DNS

Routing and DNS are two critical components of any network. Routing is like the navigation system of your network, determining how data packets get from one point to another. DNS, on the other hand, is like the phone book of the internet, translating human-readable names (like www.google.com) into numerical IP addresses that computers understand. In this chapter, we'll explore how to manage both routing and DNS using Bash, giving you the power to control the flow of traffic and ensure seamless name resolution on your network.

5.1 Static Routing

Static routing is a fundamental technique for directing network traffic. Think of it like drawing a roadmap with specific directions for how to get from one city to another. In static routing, you manually define the paths that data packets should take to reach their destination.

While dynamic routing protocols (which we'll discuss later) offer more automation and scalability, static routing still has its place in network management, especially in these scenarios:

- Small Networks: For simple networks with a limited number of devices and routes, static routing can be easier to configure and manage than dynamic routing.
- Specific Control: Static routing gives you precise control over how traffic flows through your network. You can define specific paths for certain types of traffic or prioritize certain links.

- Security: You can use static routes to restrict access to certain parts of your network or to force traffic through specific security devices like firewalls.
- Redundancy: You can configure multiple static routes to the same destination, providing backup paths in case a link or router fails.
- Connecting to Isolated Networks: Static routes are often used to connect to networks that are not directly connected to your main network.

Understanding Routing Tables

Every computer or router that participates in network communication maintains a routing table. This table is like a map that tells the device where to send data packets based on their destination IP address. Each entry in the routing table contains:

- Destination Network: The network address of the destination.
- Gateway: The IP address of the next hop router that will forward the packet towards the destination.
- Interface: The network interface that should be used to send the packet.
- Metric: A value that indicates the cost or preference of using this route.

The ip Command for Static Routing

In Linux, the ip command is your primary tool for managing static routes. Here are the essential commands:

Adding a Static Route:

Bash

```
sudo ip route add <destination_network> via
<gateway_ip> dev <interface_name>
```

- `<destination_network>`: The network address of the destination, in CIDR notation (e.g., 192.168.2.0/24).
- `<gateway_ip>`: The IP address of the next-hop router.
- `<interface_name>`: The name of the network interface to use (e.g., eth0, wlan0).

Example:

Bash

```
sudo ip route add 192.168.2.0/24 via 192.168.1.1
dev eth0
```

This command adds a route to the network 192.168.2.0/24 via the gateway 192.168.1.1[1] using the interface eth0.

Deleting a Static Route:

Bash

```
sudo ip route del <destination_network>
```

Example:

Bash

```
sudo ip route del 192.168.2.0/24
```

Viewing the Routing Table:

Bash

```
ip route show
```

This command displays the current routing table, including all static and dynamic routes.

Scripting Static Routing with Bash

You can incorporate these ip commands into your Bash scripts to automate static route management.

Example: Adding a Static Route with Error Checking

```bash
Bash

#!/bin/bash

destination="192.168.2.0/24"

gateway="192.168.1.1"

interface="eth0"

# Check if the route already exists

if ip route show | grep -q "$destination via
$gateway"; then

  echo "Route to $destination already exists."

else

  # Add the static route

  sudo ip route add $destination via $gateway dev
$interface

  echo "Static route to $destination via $gateway
added."

fi
```

This script checks if the route already exists before adding it.

Real-World Examples:

- Connecting to a Guest Network: In a hotel or conference center, you might need to add a static route to access the internet through their guest Wi-Fi network.

- Configuring a VPN Connection: When you connect to a VPN, static routes are often added to direct traffic through the VPN tunnel.
- Setting up a Site-to-Site VPN: Static routes are used to define the networks that should be accessible through the VPN connection between two sites.

Exercises:

1. Add a static route on your system to a specific destination network (if you have access to multiple networks).
2. Write a Bash script that adds a static route and then verifies that the route has been added correctly by checking the routing table.
3. Write a Bash script that deletes a static route based on the destination network provided as a command-line argument.

5.2 Dynamic Routing

Dynamic routing is a more sophisticated approach to managing network traffic. Think of it like using a GPS navigation system that automatically adjusts your route based on real-time traffic conditions. Dynamic routing allows your network to adapt to changes, find the best paths for data packets, and maintain connectivity even if links or devices fail.

While static routing offers simplicity and control, it can become cumbersome and inefficient in larger, more complex networks. This is where dynamic routing shines:

- Scalability: Dynamic routing protocols are designed to handle large networks with many devices and complex topologies. They can automatically discover new routes and adapt to changes in the network.
- Adaptability: Dynamic routing allows your network to self-heal and reroute traffic around failures. If a link goes

down or a router becomes unavailable, the routing protocol will automatically find alternative paths to ensure connectivity.

- Efficiency: Dynamic routing protocols calculate the best paths for data packets based on various metrics, such as bandwidth, latency, and hop count. This helps to optimize network performance and avoid congestion.
- Reduced Administrative Overhead: Dynamic routing reduces the need for manual configuration of routes, especially in large networks where static routing would be impractical.

Dynamic Routing Protocols

Dynamic routing relies on routing protocols, which are sets of rules that routers use to exchange routing information and automatically update their routing tables. Here are some of the most common dynamic routing protocols:

- RIP (Routing Information Protocol): This is one of the oldest and simplest routing protocols. It uses hop count as the metric to determine the best path. RIP is easy to configure but has limitations in terms of scalability and convergence time (the time it takes for routers to agree on the best routes).
- OSPF (Open Shortest Path First): This is a more advanced link-state routing protocol that uses a hierarchical structure to represent the network. OSPF calculates the best paths based on link costs, which can be configured to represent bandwidth, latency, or other factors. It's more efficient and scalable than RIP.
- BGP (Border Gateway Protocol): This is the protocol used to route traffic between different autonomous systems (AS) on the internet. An AS is a network or group of networks under a single administrative domain. BGP is essential for the internet's functionality, allowing different networks to

exchange routing information and ensuring that data can reach its destination across the globe.

How Dynamic Routing Works

Routers running dynamic routing protocols exchange routing information with their neighbors. This information includes:

- Reachable Networks: The networks that the router can reach.
- Metrics: The cost or distance to reach those networks.

Routers use this information to build their routing tables, which they then use to forward data packets. When a change occurs in the network (like a link failure), routers propagate this information to their neighbors, triggering a recalculation of routes. This process ensures that the network can adapt to changes and maintain connectivity.

Configuring Dynamic Routing

Configuring dynamic routing involves setting up routing daemons (software that runs on routers to implement routing protocols) and configuring them with the appropriate routing protocols and parameters. This process varies depending on the routing protocol and the specific router or operating system you're using.

Some common routing daemons include:

- quagga: A routing software suite that supports various routing protocols, including RIP, OSPF, and BGP.
- bird: Another popular routing daemon with support for multiple protocols.

Scripting Dynamic Routing Management with Bash

While the detailed configuration of dynamic routing is often done through configuration files or specialized tools, you can use Bash scripts to automate some aspects of dynamic routing management, such as:

- Starting and Stopping Routing Daemons: You can write scripts to start or stop routing daemons on your routers.
- Monitoring Routing Table Updates: You can use scripts to periodically check the routing table and send alerts if there are significant changes or unexpected routes.
- Collecting Routing Information: You can use scripts to gather routing information from routers and store it for analysis or troubleshooting.

Real-World Examples:

- Enterprise Networks: Large enterprise networks rely heavily on dynamic routing protocols like OSPF to manage their complex internal networks and ensure efficient routing of traffic.
- Internet Service Providers (ISPs): ISPs use BGP to exchange routing information with other ISPs and route internet traffic across their networks.
- Data Centers: Data centers use dynamic routing to manage the flow of traffic between servers, storage devices, and network equipment.

Exercises:

1. Research the quagga or bird routing daemons and learn how to install and configure them on a Linux system.
2. Write a Bash script that starts and stops a routing daemon.
3. Write a Bash script that monitors the routing table for changes and logs any new routes that are added.

Understanding dynamic routing and its associated protocols, you gain a deeper understanding of how large networks operate and how to manage them effectively. While the detailed configuration of dynamic routing might require specialized tools, Bash scripting can still play a role in automating tasks and monitoring routing information.

5.3 DNS Server Configuration

Think of a DNS server as the address book of your network, or even the internet. It translates those easy-to-remember names like google.com into the IP addresses that computers use to communicate, like 172.217.160.142. Without DNS, we'd all be memorizing long strings of numbers!

Setting up a DNS server gives you more control over name resolution in your network and can even provide some cool features like ad-blocking or internal domain management.

Why Set Up a DNS Server?

- Control: You have complete control over how domain names are resolved within your network.
- Privacy: You can choose not to rely on third-party DNS servers, keeping your DNS queries private.
- Performance: You can potentially improve name resolution speed for your local network.
- Reliability: You can configure your server to be more resilient to outages than relying on external DNS servers.
- Customization: You can implement features like internal domain names, ad-blocking, or custom DNS records.

Choosing DNS Server Software

There are several popular DNS server software options available, each with its own strengths and weaknesses:

- BIND (Berkeley Internet Name Domain): This is one of the oldest and most widely used DNS server implementations. It's robust and feature-rich, but it can be complex to configure.

- Dnsmasq: This is a lightweight and easy-to-configure DNS server that is often used in home and small office networks. It also provides DHCP and TFTP services.
- Unbound: This is a secure and validating DNS resolver that focuses on security and privacy. It performs DNSSEC validation to ensure the authenticity of DNS responses.

Basic DNS Server Configuration

The exact configuration steps will vary depending on the DNS server software you choose. However, the general process involves:

1. Installation: Install the DNS server software on your Linux system.
2. Configuration: Edit the configuration file to define:
   - Listening Interfaces: Specify the network interfaces on which the server should listen for DNS requests.
   - Forwarders: If you want your server to forward queries it cannot resolve to external DNS servers (like Google Public DNS), you can specify their IP addresses.
   - Access Control: You can configure access control lists (ACLs) to restrict who can query your DNS server.
3. Zone Definition: Define the DNS zones that your server will be responsible for. A zone is a portion of the DNS namespace, typically corresponding to a domain name (e.g., example.com).
4. Resource Records: Add resource records to your zone files. These records store information about domain names, such as:
   - A records: Map domain names to IPv4 addresses.
   - AAAA records: Map domain names to IPv6 addresses.
   - CNAME records: Create aliases[1] for domain names.
   - MX records: Specify mail servers for a domain.

- NS records: Delegate subdomains to other name servers.

Example BIND Configuration (named.conf.options):

```
options {

        directory "/var/cache/bind";

        forwarders {

                8.8.8.8;

                8.8.4.4;

        };

        allow-query { any; };

};
```

Example BIND Zone File (example.com.zone):

```
$TTL 1D

@       IN SOA  ns1.example.com.
hostmaster.example.com. (

                        2024120901 ;
Serial

                        3H          ;
Refresh

                        15M         ;
Retry
```

```
                                    1W            ;
Expire

                                    1D )          ;
Negative Cache TTL

;

@               IN      NS      ns1.example.com.

ns1             IN      A       192.168.1.10

www             IN      A       192.168.1.20
```

Scripting DNS Server Management with Bash

You can use Bash scripts to automate various aspects of DNS server management:

- Adding and Updating DNS Records: You can write scripts to dynamically add or update DNS records based on information from other sources or in response to network events.
- Checking DNS Server Status: You can use scripts to monitor the health of your DNS server and send alerts if there are any problems.
- Generating DNS Zone Files: You can write scripts to generate zone files based on information from databases or configuration files.

Real-World Examples:

- Internal DNS for a Company: You can set up a DNS server to manage internal domain names and provide name resolution for devices within your company network.
- Ad Blocking: You can configure your DNS server to block requests to known ad servers, reducing unwanted ads and improving browsing experience for users on your network.

- Dynamic DNS: You can use a dynamic DNS service to update your DNS records automatically when your public IP address changes, allowing you to access your home network or servers from anywhere.

Exercises:

1. Install and configure a DNS server software like BIND or Dnsmasq on a Linux system.
2. Create a simple zone file for a domain name and configure your DNS server to serve that zone.
3. Write a Bash script that adds a new A record to your zone file and then reloads the DNS server to apply the changes.

5.4 DNS Client Configuration

The devices on your network that need to look up domain names and translate them into IP addresses. Think of your computer, smartphone, or even your smart refrigerator as a DNS client. Every time you type a website address in your browser or use an app that connects to the internet, your device relies on DNS to find the correct server.

Why Configure DNS Clients?

Proper DNS client configuration is crucial for:

- Name Resolution: Ensuring that your devices can reliably resolve domain names to IP addresses. This is essential for accessing websites, sending emails, and using online services.
- Performance: Choosing fast and reliable DNS servers can improve name resolution speed and overall network performance.
- Security: Using secure DNS servers can protect your privacy and prevent DNS spoofing or hijacking attacks.

- Content Filtering: You can configure your DNS clients to use DNS servers that provide content filtering, blocking access to unwanted websites or content.

/etc/resolv.conf - The Traditional Way

In Linux, the traditional way to configure DNS clients is by editing the /etc/resolv.conf file. This file contains a list of DNS server IP addresses that the client should use for name resolution.

Example /etc/resolv.conf **file:**

```
nameserver 8.8.8.8

nameserver 8.8.4.4
```

This configures the client to use Google's public DNS servers (8.8.8.8 and 8.8.4.4). You can add multiple nameserver entries, and the client will try them in order until it gets a response.

systemd-resolved - The Modern Approach

In most modern Linux distributions, systemd-resolved is a system service that provides network name resolution. It acts as a local DNS cache and can forward queries to external DNS servers.

Configuring systemd-resolved

You can configure systemd-resolved using the resolvectl command.

- **Setting DNS Servers:**

```
Bash

sudo resolvectl dns eth0 8.8.8.8 8.8.4.4
```

This sets the DNS servers for the interface etho to Google Public DNS.

- **Viewing DNS Configuration:**

Bash

```
resolvectl status
```

This displays the current DNS configuration, including the DNS servers, domains, and link status.

- **Flushing the DNS Cache:**

Bash

```
sudo resolvectl flush-caches
```

This clears the local DNS cache, forcing the resolver to query the DNS servers for fresh information.

DHCP and DNS

In many networks, DNS server information is provided automatically by DHCP. When your device obtains an IP address from a DHCP server, it usually also receives the IP addresses of the DNS servers to use.

Scripting DNS Client Configuration with Bash

You can use Bash scripts to automate DNS client configuration.

Example: Setting DNS Servers with resolv.conf

Bash

```
#!/bin/bash

nameserver1="1.1.1.1"  # Cloudflare DNS

nameserver2="1.0.0.1"

# Update resolv.conf
```

```bash
echo "nameserver $nameserver" > /etc/resolv.conf

echo "nameserver $nameserver2" >>
/etc/resolv.conf

echo "DNS servers updated in /etc/resolv.conf"
```

Example: Setting DNS Servers with systemd-resolved

```bash
Bash

#!/bin/bash

interface="wlan0"

nameserver1="9.9.9.9"  # Quad9 DNS

nameserver2="149.112.112.112"

# Update DNS servers for the interface

sudo resolvectl dns $interface $nameserver1
$nameserver2

echo "DNS servers updated for $interface using
systemd-resolved"
```

Real-World Examples:

- Parental Controls: You can configure your home network to use a DNS server that provides parental controls, filtering out inappropriate content for children.
- Ad Blocking: You can use DNS servers that block ads, providing a cleaner browsing experience.
- Improving Privacy: You can use privacy-focused DNS servers that do not track your DNS queries.
- Accessing Geo-Restricted Content: You can use DNS servers located in different countries to bypass geo-restrictions and access content that might be blocked in your region.

Exercises:

1. Manually configure the DNS servers on your system by editing the /etc/resolv.conf file.
2. Use resolvectl to set the DNS servers for a specific network interface.
3. Write a Bash script that switches between different sets of DNS servers based on a command-line argument or a configuration file.
4. Research different public DNS services (Google Public DNS, Cloudflare DNS, Quad9) and compare their features and performance.

Mastering DNS client configuration with Bash, you can ensure reliable name resolution, improve network performance, enhance privacy, and even implement content filtering. This is an essential skill for managing any device that connects to the internet.

Chapter 6: Firewall Management with Bash

Let's discuss firewalls and how you can manage them with the power of Bash. Think of a firewall as a security guard for your network, controlling the flow of traffic in and out of your system. It acts like a filter, allowing or blocking connections based on rules you define. With Bash, you can automate the configuration of these rules, making your network security more robust and adaptable.

6.1 Introduction to Firewalls

A firewall is a network security system that monitors and controls incoming and outgoing network traffic based on predetermined security rules. It acts as a barrier between your[2] trusted internal network and untrusted external networks, such as the internet.

Firewalls work by inspecting network packets, which are the small units of data that travel across networks. They analyze the contents of these packets, looking at information like the source and destination IP addresses, port numbers, and protocols. Based on this analysis, the firewall decides whether to allow or block the packet.

Why are Firewalls Important?

Firewalls are essential for protecting your systems and data from various threats, including:

- Unauthorized Access: Firewalls prevent unauthorized users from accessing your computer or network. This helps to protect sensitive data, prevent malware infections, and stop hackers from taking control of your systems.

113

- Malicious Traffic: Firewalls can block malicious traffic, such as denial-of-service attacks, port scans, and attempts to exploit vulnerabilities in your systems.
- Data Leakage: Firewalls can prevent sensitive data from leaving your network without authorization.
- Network Segmentation: Firewalls can be used to isolate different parts of your network, limiting the impact of security breaches. For example, you can use a firewall to separate your internal network from a guest Wi-Fi network.

Types of Firewalls

There are several types of firewalls, each with its own strengths and weaknesses:

- Packet Filtering Firewalls: These are the most basic type of firewall. They operate at the network layer and examine individual packets, making decisions based on simple criteria like source/destination IP address, port number, and protocol. They are relatively fast and efficient but have limited capabilities in terms of analyzing complex traffic patterns or application-level behavior.
- Stateful Firewalls: These firewalls are more sophisticated than packet filtering firewalls. They keep track of the state of network connections, allowing them to make more intelligent decisions about traffic filtering. For example, a stateful firewall can return traffic for outgoing connections that it initiated, but block unsolicited incoming connections.
- Application-Level Firewalls (Proxy Firewalls): These firewalls operate at the application layer and can filter traffic based on the application or service being used. They can, for example, block access to specific websites or applications, or scan traffic for malicious content. Application-level firewalls provide more granular control over network traffic but can be more resource-intensive.
- Next-Generation Firewalls (NGFWs): These are advanced firewalls that combine features of traditional firewalls with

additional security capabilities, such as intrusion prevention systems (IPS), deep packet inspection (DPI), and malware scanning. NGFWs provide comprehensive protection against a wide range of threats.

How Firewalls Work with Other Security Measures

Firewalls are just one piece of the security puzzle. They should be used in conjunction with other security measures, such as:

- Intrusion Detection/Prevention Systems (IDS/IPS): These systems monitor network traffic for suspicious activity and can block or alert on potential attacks.
- Antivirus Software: This software protects against malware infections by scanning files and detecting known viruses, worms, and Trojans.
- Strong Passwords: Using strong, unique passwords for all your accounts helps to prevent unauthorized access.
- Regular Software Updates: Keeping your software up to date ensures that you have the latest security patches and fixes.

Real-World Examples

- Home Networks: Most home routers include a built-in firewall that protects your home network from internet threats.
- Business Networks: Businesses use firewalls to protect their internal networks from external attacks and to control access to sensitive data.
- Cloud Environments: Cloud providers use firewalls to secure their infrastructure and protect customer data.
- Web Applications: Web application firewalls (WAFs) are used to protect web applications from attacks like SQL injection and cross-site scripting (XSS).

Exercises

1. Check if your computer has a firewall enabled. If you're using Linux, you can use the firewall-cmd --state command to check the status of firewalld.
2. Research the different types of firewalls available for your operating system.
3. Think about the security needs of your home or work network and how a firewall can help to protect it.

By understanding the role of firewalls in network security, you can make informed decisions about how to protect your systems and data from unauthorized access and malicious activity.

6.2 Working with iptables

iptables is a packet filtering firewall that works by examining individual network packets and comparing them against a set of rules. These rules are organized into chains and tables, providing a flexible framework for managing network security.

Basic iptables Commands

Before we start building complex firewall rules, let's familiarize ourselves with some basic iptables commands:

- iptables -L: This command lists the current firewall rules. You'll see a table-like output showing the chains (INPUT, OUTPUT, FORWARD), the rule number, the match criteria, and the action (ACCEPT, DROP, REJECT).
- iptables -A <chain> <rule>: This command appends a new rule to the specified chain. For example, to allow incoming HTTP traffic (port 80), you would use:

Bash

```bash
sudo iptables -A INPUT -p tcp --dport 80 -j
ACCEPT
```

- iptables -I <chain> <rule_number> <rule>: This command inserts a new rule at a specific position in the chain. For example, to insert a rule at the beginning of the INPUT chain to block traffic from a specific IP address, you would use:

Bash

```bash
sudo iptables -I INPUT 1 -s 192.168.1.10 -j DROP
```

- iptables -D <chain> <rule>: This command deletes a rule from the specified chain. You can either specify the rule number or the complete rule definition. For example, to delete a rule that allows SSH traffic (port 22), you would use:

Bash

```bash
sudo iptables -D INPUT -p tcp --dport 22 -j
ACCEPT
```

- iptables -F: This command flushes all rules from all chains. It's like resetting the firewall to its default state.
- iptables -P <chain> <target>: This command sets the default policy for a chain. The default policy is the action that is taken if no other rule matches. For example, to set the default policy for the INPUT chain to DROP (block all traffic by default), you would use:

Bash

```
sudo iptables -P INPUT DROP
```

iptables Chains

iptables uses chains to organize firewall rules. The three main chains are:

- INPUT: This chain handles incoming traffic to your system. Rules in this chain determine what happens to packets that are destined for your computer.
- OUTPUT: This chain handles outgoing traffic from your system. Rules in this chain determine what happens to packets that originate from your computer.
- FORWARD: This chain handles traffic that is being routed through your system (if your computer is acting as a router).

iptables Tables

iptables also uses tables to group rules based on their function. The main tables are:

- **filter:** This is the default table and is used for general packet filtering. It contains the INPUT, OUTPUT, and FORWARD chains.
- **nat:** This table is used for Network Address Translation (NAT), which allows you to modify the source or destination IP addresses of packets. This is commonly used for port forwarding and network address translation.
- **mangle:** This table is used for specialized packet alteration, such as modifying the TTL (Time-to-Live) of packets or marking packets for Quality of Service (QoS).

Building Firewall Rules

An iptables rule consists of several parts:

- Chain: The chain to which the rule belongs (INPUT, OUTPUT, or FORWARD).

- Match: The criteria that the packet must match for the rule to apply. This can include the source/destination IP address, port number, protocol, and other factors.
- Target: The action to take if the packet matches the rule. This can be ACCEPT (allow the packet), DROP (silently discard the packet), or REJECT (send an error message back to the sender).

Example Rule:

Bash

```
iptables -A INPUT -p tcp --dport 80 -j ACCEPT
```

This rule appends a new rule to the INPUT chain. It matches TCP packets destined for port 80 (HTTP) and accepts them.

Real-World Examples

- Allowing Web Traffic: To allow incoming web traffic to your server, you would add a rule to the INPUT chain to accept TCP traffic on port 80 (HTTP) and port 443 (HTTPS).
- Blocking Specific IP Addresses: To block traffic from a known malicious IP address, you would add a rule to the INPUT chain to drop all traffic from that IP address.
- Setting up a DMZ: To create a demilitarized zone (DMZ) for a web server, you would use iptables to forward traffic on specific ports (e.g., 80 and 443) to the web server's IP address.

Exercises

1. Use iptables -L to list the current firewall rules on your system.
2. Add a rule to the INPUT chain to allow SSH traffic (port 22) from a specific IP address.
3. Add a rule to the OUTPUT chain to block all traffic to a specific domain name.

4. Research the iptables nat table and learn how to use it for port forwarding.

6.3 Working with firewalld

Firewalld is a more modern and user-friendly way to manage firewalls in Linux. Think of firewalld as a higher-level interface built on top of iptables. It provides a simpler way to configure firewall rules using concepts like zones and services, making it easier to manage your network security.

Why use firewalld?

- Simplicity: firewalld offers a more intuitive and user-friendly interface compared to iptables. It uses zones and services to simplify firewall management, making it easier to understand and configure.
- Dynamic Management: firewalld allows for dynamic adjustments to firewall rules without disrupting existing connections. You can add or remove rules without restarting the entire firewall.
- Flexibility: firewalld supports network zones, allowing you to define different sets of rules for different network environments (e.g., home, public, work).
- Integration with systemd: firewalld is well-integrated with systemd, the init system used in most modern Linux distributions.

firewalld Concepts

- Zones: firewalld uses zones to define different sets of firewall rules. Think of zones as different security levels or trust levels for different networks. Some common zones include:
    - public: For use in public areas, with minimal allowed services.

- home: For use in home areas, with more relaxed rules.
- internal: For use in internal networks, with trusted devices.
- work: For use in work environments, with specific rules for work-related services.
- dmz: For servers in a demilitarized zone (DMZ), which is a more exposed part of the network.
- Services: firewalld provides predefined services that represent common network applications (like HTTP, SSH, FTP). You can easily add or remove these services from zones to control access.
- Interfaces: You assign network interfaces to specific zones. This determines which set of firewall rules applies to traffic on that interface.

Basic firewalld Commands

Here are some essential firewalld commands:

- firewall-cmd --list-all-zones: This command lists all available firewall zones on your system.
- firewall-cmd --get-active-zones: This command shows you which zones are currently active and which interfaces are assigned to them.
- firewall-cmd --get-default-zone: This command displays the default zone that is assigned to new network interfaces.
- firewall-cmd --set-default-zone=<zone>: This command allows you to change the default zone.
- firewall-cmd --zone=<zone> --add-service=<service>: This command adds a predefined service to the specified zone. For example, to allow HTTP traffic in the public zone, you would use:

Bash

```
sudo firewall-cmd --zone=public
--add-service=http
```

- firewall-cmd --zone=<zone> --remove-service=<service>: This command removes a service from the specified zone.
- firewall-cmd --zone=<zone> --add-port=<port>/<protocol>: This command adds a specific port and protocol to the allowed services in a zone. For example, to allow SSH traffic in the public zone, you would use:

Bash

```
sudo firewall-cmd --zone=public --add-port=22/tcp
```

- firewall-cmd --zone=<zone> --remove-port=<port>/<protocol>: This command removes a specific port and protocol from the allowed services in a zone.
- firewall-cmd --reload: This command reloads the firewall configuration. Any changes you make to the firewall rules will not take effect until you reload the firewall.
- firewall-cmd --permanent --add-service=<service>: To make your changes persistent across reboots, use the --permanent flag. For example:

Bash

```
sudo firewall-cmd --permanent --zone=public
--add-service=https

sudo firewall-cmd --reload
```

Real-World Examples

- Securing a Home Network: You can use firewalld to configure your home network with a "home" zone for trusted devices and a "public" zone for guest access, limiting the access that guest devices have to your internal network.
- Setting Up a Web Server: You can place your web server in a "dmz" zone with rules that allow HTTP and HTTPS traffic, while blocking other types of connections.
- Controlling Application Access: You can use firewalld to control which applications on your system are allowed to access the network. For example, you can block access to the internet for specific applications that you don't want to communicate with external servers.

Exercises

1. Use firewall-cmd --get-active-zones to see which zones are active on your system.
2. Add the SSH service to the public zone using firewalld.
3. Create a new zone called "restricted" and add a rule to block all outgoing traffic from that zone.
4. Research the different predefined services available in firewalld and experiment with adding and removing them from different zones.

6.4 Advanced Firewall Rules

Let's discuss how to create more sophisticated and powerful firewall rules using iptables and firewalld. We'll go beyond the basics and learn how to filter traffic based on a wider range of criteria, giving you more granular control over your network security.

iptables Advanced Rules

iptables offers a rich set of options for creating advanced firewall rules. Here are some key techniques:

- **Filtering by Source/Destination IP Address and Port:** You can specify the source and destination IP addresses and ports to filter traffic very precisely.

Bash

```
sudo iptables -A INPUT -s 192.168.1.10 -p tcp
--dport 80 -j ACCEPT  # Allow HTTP from a
specific IP

sudo iptables -A OUTPUT -d 10.0.0.0/24 -j DROP #
Block all outgoing traffic to a network
```

- **Filtering by Protocol:** You can filter traffic based on the protocol (TCP, UDP, ICMP).[1]

Bash

```
sudo iptables -A INPUT -p icmp -j DROP  # Block
all ICMP traffic (ping)

sudo iptables -A FORWARD -p udp --dport 53 -j
ACCEPT # Allow DNS traffic (UDP port 53)
```

- **Filtering by Interface:** You can specify the network interface on which the rule should apply.

Bash

```
sudo iptables -A INPUT -i eth0 -j ACCEPT  # Allow
all traffic on eth0
```

```
sudo iptables -A FORWARD -o wlan0 -j DROP # Block
all forwarding traffic on wlan0
```

- **Filtering by Connection State:** This is a powerful feature of iptables that allows you to filter traffic based on the state of the connection.

```
Bash
```

```
sudo iptables -A INPUT -m conntrack --ctstate
ESTABLISHED,RELATED -j ACCEPT # Allow established
and related connections

sudo iptables -A INPUT -m conntrack --ctstate NEW
-p tcp --dport 22 -j ACCEPT # Allow new SSH
connections
```

- **Filtering by Time:** You can use the time module to filter traffic based on the time of day or day of the week.

```
Bash
```

```
sudo iptables -A INPUT -m time --timestart 08:00
--timestop 17:00 -j ACCEPT # Allow traffic only
during working hours

sudo iptables -A INPUT -m time --weekdays
Mon,Tue,Wed,Thu,Fri -j ACCEPT # Allow traffic
only on weekdays
```

- **Filtering by User:** You can use the owner module to filter traffic based on the user who initiated the connection.

Bash

```
sudo iptables -A OUTPUT -m owner --uid-owner
alice -j ACCEPT # Allow outgoing traffic from
user alice
```

- Logging: You can use the LOG target to log packets that match a rule. This is useful for auditing and troubleshooting.

Bash

```
sudo iptables -A INPUT -p tcp --dport 80 -j LOG
--log-prefix "HTTP Access: " # Log all HTTP
requests
```

firewalld Advanced Rules

While firewalld focuses on simplicity, it also provides ways to create more advanced rules:

- Rich Language: firewalld offers a rich language for defining services, allowing you to specify ports, protocols, source/destination addresses, and other criteria.
- Direct Interface: You can use the firewall-cmd --direct option to pass raw iptables commands to firewalld, giving you access to the full power of iptables if needed.
- IP Sets: firewalld supports IP sets, which are dynamic collections of IP addresses. You can use IP sets to create rules that match against a group of IP addresses that can change over time.[2]

Real-World Examples

- Rate Limiting: You can use iptables to limit the rate of incoming connections on a specific port, preventing denial-of-service attacks.

- Blocking Specific Countries: You can use iptables with geoip databases to block traffic from specific countries.
- Creating a Time-Based Firewall: You can use firewalld to create a firewall that allows different services during different times of the day. For example, you might allow SSH access only during working hours.

Exercises

1. Use iptables to create a rule that allows SSH connections only from a specific IP address and only during working hours.
2. Use firewalld to create a rule that blocks all traffic to a specific domain name.
3. Research how to use IP sets with firewalld to create dynamic firewall rules.
4. Explore the iptables mangle table and learn how to use it to modify packet headers.

By mastering advanced firewall rules with iptables and firewalld, you can create highly customized and effective firewall policies to protect your network from a wide range of threats. This is a valuable skill for any security-conscious system administrator.

6.5 Scripting Firewall Policies

This is where you can combine the power of iptables or firewalld with the flexibility of Bash to create dynamic and responsive firewall configurations. Think of it like writing a set of instructions for your firewall, allowing it to adapt to changing conditions and enforce complex security rules.

Why Script Firewall Policies?

Scripting firewall policies offers several benefits:

- Automation: You can automate repetitive tasks, such as adding or removing firewall rules based on specific events or schedules.
- Flexibility: You can create dynamic firewall rules that adapt to changing network conditions or security threats.[1]
- Consistency: You can ensure consistent firewall configuration across multiple systems.
- Maintainability: You can store your firewall policies in scripts, making them easier to manage, version control, and share.
- Efficiency: You can quickly implement complex firewall configurations with just a few lines of code.

Scripting with iptables

You can use Bash scripts to execute iptables commands and manage your firewall rules.

Example: Blocking an IP Address

Bash

```bash
#!/bin/bash

# Get the IP address to block from the command
line

ip_to_block=$1

# Check if an IP address was provided

if [ -z "$ip_to_block" ]; then

  echo "Usage: $0 <ip_address>"

  exit 1

fi
```

```bash
# Block the IP address

sudo iptables -A INPUT -s $ip_to_block -j DROP

echo "Blocked IP address: $ip_to_block"
```

This script takes an IP address as an argument and adds an iptables rule to block incoming traffic from that address.

Example: Allowing SSH Access During Working Hours

Bash

```bash
#!/bin/bash

# Allow SSH access only during working hours (8 AM to 5 PM)

sudo iptables -A INPUT -p tcp -m time --timestart 08:00 --timestop 17:00 --dport 22 -j ACCEPT

# Block SSH access outside working hours

sudo iptables -A INPUT -p tcp --dport 22 -j DROP
```

This script uses the time module to allow SSH access only during specific hours.

Scripting with firewalld

You can also use Bash scripts to interact with firewalld and manage your firewall zones and services.

Example: Adding a Service to a Zone

Bash

```bash
#!/bin/bash

zone="public"
```

```bash
service="https"

# Add the service to the zone

sudo firewall-cmd --permanent --zone=$zone
--add-service=$service

sudo firewall-cmd --reload

echo "Added service $service to zone $zone"
```

This script adds a service (HTTPS) to the specified zone (public) and reloads the firewall.

Example: Blocking a Port in a Zone

Bash

```bash
#!/bin/bash

zone="dmz"

port="25/tcp"  # Block SMTP traffic

# Remove the port from the zone

sudo firewall-cmd --permanent --zone=$zone
--remove-port=$port

sudo firewall-cmd --reload

echo "Blocked port $port in zone $zone"
```

This script removes a specific port (SMTP) from the specified zone (dmz).

Real-World Examples

- **Dynamically Blocking IPs:** You can write a script that monitors log files for suspicious activity and automatically blocks IP addresses that exhibit malicious behavior.
- **Automated Firewall Updates:** You can create scripts that automatically update your firewall rules based on changes to your network configuration or security policies.[2]
- **Scheduled Firewall Tasks:** You can use cron jobs to schedule regular firewall tasks, such as nightly updates or weekly backups of your firewall configuration.

Exercises

1. Write a Bash script that takes an IP address as an argument and blocks it using iptables.
2. Write a Bash script that allows HTTP and HTTPS access in the public zone using firewalld.
3. Create a Bash script that blocks all outgoing traffic on weekends using iptables.
4. Research how to use cron jobs to schedule regular firewall tasks.

Mastering scripting firewall policies with Bash, you can automate your network security, create dynamic firewall configurations, and ensure that your systems are protected from evolving threats.[3] This is a valuable skill for any system administrator or security professional who wants to manage their firewall efficiently and effectively.

Chapter 7: Network Monitoring Scripts

Let's discuss network monitoring and how you can use Bash scripts to keep a watchful eye on your network. Think of network monitoring as the health checkup for your network. It's like regularly taking your network's temperature, checking its pulse, and making sure everything is running smoothly. With Bash, you can automate these checks, gather valuable performance data, and even detect potential problems before they cause major disruptions.

7.1 Monitoring Bandwidth Usage

Think of bandwidth as the capacity of your network connection, like the size of a water pipe. The more data you transmit and receive, the more bandwidth you consume. Monitoring bandwidth usage is crucial for understanding how your network is being utilized, identifying potential bottlenecks, and ensuring that you have enough capacity to support your applications and services.[1]

Why Monitor Bandwidth Usage?

- Identify Bottlenecks: If you're experiencing slow network performance, monitoring bandwidth can help you identify which applications or devices are consuming the most bandwidth and causing congestion.[2]
- Capacity Planning: By tracking bandwidth usage over time, you can predict future needs and plan for upgrades or expansions to your network infrastructure.[3]
- Cost Optimization: Monitoring bandwidth can help you identify unnecessary or excessive usage, allowing you to optimize your network costs and potentially reduce your internet bill.[4]

- Security: Unusual spikes in bandwidth usage can sometimes indicate malicious activity, such as denial-of-service attacks or data exfiltration.[5]

Tools for Monitoring Bandwidth

Linux provides several powerful tools for monitoring bandwidth usage:[6]

- vnstat: This command-line tool provides detailed statistics about network traffic on your interfaces.[7] It can track bandwidth usage over time, showing you daily, monthly, and even yearly statistics.[8] It's particularly useful for long-term monitoring and trend analysis.

Bash

```
vnstat -i eth0
```

This command will display bandwidth statistics for the interface etho, including total data transferred, average transfer rates, and historical data.

- iftop: This tool displays a real-time view of bandwidth usage on your network interfaces.[9] It shows you which processes are using the most bandwidth and which hosts they are communicating with. It's great for identifying bandwidth hogs and understanding network traffic patterns in real-time.[10]
- bmon: This is another tool that provides a real-time view of bandwidth usage, with various options for displaying data graphically or in text mode.[11] It offers more customization options than iftop and can be useful for visualizing network traffic patterns.

Scripting Bandwidth Monitoring with Bash

You can use these tools in your Bash scripts to automate bandwidth monitoring and create custom monitoring solutions.

Example: Logging Bandwidth Usage with vnstat

```
Bash

#!/bin/bash

interface="eth0"

logfile="bandwidth_usage.log"

# Get daily bandwidth usage from vnstat

bandwidth=$(vnstat -i $interface --days | grep "today" | awk '{print $8}')

# Log the bandwidth usage with timestamp

echo "$(date) - Bandwidth usage on $interface: $bandwidth" >> $logfile
```

This script retrieves the daily bandwidth usage for the specified interface using vnstat and logs it to a file with a timestamp. You can then use this log file to track bandwidth usage over time and identify trends or anomalies.

Example: Monitoring Bandwidth Usage with iftop

While iftop is primarily an interactive tool, you can use it in scripts with some limitations. For example, you can capture its output for a specific duration and then analyze it.

```
Bash

#!/bin/bash
```

```
interface="wlan0"

duration="10"  # Monitor for 10 seconds

# Capture iftop output for the specified duration

iftop -i $interface -t -s $duration >
iftop_output.txt

# Analyze the output (e.g., extract top talkers)

# ...
```

Real-World Examples

- Network Capacity Planning: You can use vnstat to track bandwidth usage trends over time and predict when you might need to upgrade your internet connection or network infrastructure.
- Troubleshooting Network Slowdowns: If you experience slow network performance, you can use iftop to identify which applications or devices are consuming the most bandwidth and investigate further.
- Monitoring Server Bandwidth: You can monitor the bandwidth usage of your servers to ensure that they have enough capacity to handle client requests and prevent performance issues.
- Detecting DDoS Attacks: Sudden and unexpected spikes in bandwidth usage can sometimes indicate a denial-of-service (DDoS) attack.[12] You can use monitoring scripts to detect such anomalies and trigger alerts.

Exercises

1. Install vnstat and use it to monitor the bandwidth usage on your network interface for a few days. Analyze the output and observe the traffic patterns.

2. Write a Bash script that uses vnstat to log hourly bandwidth usage to a file.
3. Install iftop and use it to observe real-time bandwidth usage on your network. Identify the top talkers (applications or hosts using the most bandwidth).
4. Write a Bash script that captures iftop output for a specific duration and then extracts the IP addresses of the top 10 bandwidth consumers.

By mastering bandwidth monitoring with Bash, you gain the ability to understand your network traffic patterns, identify potential bottlenecks, and make informed decisions about network capacity planning and optimization. This is a crucial skill for any network administrator or engineer who wants to maintain a high-performing and efficient network.

7.2 Checking Network Connectivity

Checking network connectivity is one of the most fundamental tasks in network management. Think of it like checking the pulse of your network – you want to make sure that all the critical devices are reachable and responding. With Bash, you can automate these checks, ensuring that you're always aware of the status of your network connections.[1]

Why Check Network Connectivity?

- Early Problem Detection: Regularly checking connectivity allows you to detect network problems early on, before they escalate and cause major disruptions.[2]
- Troubleshooting: When you encounter network issues, connectivity checks are the first step in diagnosing the problem.[3] They help you pinpoint where the connection is failing and narrow down the possible causes.[4]
- Monitoring Critical Services: You can monitor the availability of critical servers, websites, or network devices to ensure that they are always accessible.

- Automated Failover: You can use connectivity checks to trigger automated failover mechanisms, switching to backup systems or connections if a primary one fails.

Tools for Checking Connectivity

Bash provides several tools for checking network connectivity:[5]

- ping: This is the most basic and widely used tool for checking connectivity to a host.[6] It sends ICMP echo requests to the target host and waits for ICMP echo replies.[7] If replies are received, it indicates that the host is reachable.

Bash

```
ping -c 4 www.google.com
```

This command sends 4 echo requests to www.google.com and displays the results, including the round-trip time and packet loss.

- fping: This is a more advanced version of ping that can ping multiple hosts simultaneously. It's more efficient than ping for checking the status of many hosts.

Bash

```
fping -c 4 host1.example.com host2.example.com
host3.example.com
```

This command sends 4 echo requests to each of the specified hosts.[8]

- nc (netcat): This versatile tool can be used to test connectivity on specific TCP or UDP ports.[9]

Bash

```
nc -zv www.example.com 80
```

This command checks if port 80 (HTTP) is open on www.example.com.

Scripting Connectivity Checks with Bash

You can use these tools in your Bash scripts to automate connectivity checks and create custom monitoring solutions.

Example: Checking Multiple Hosts with fping

Bash

```
#!/bin/bash

hosts=("www.google.com" "www.amazon.com"
"192.168.1.10")

# Ping each host and check the result

for host in "${hosts[@]}"; do

  if fping -c 4 $host > /dev/null 2>&1; then

    echo "$host is reachable"

  else

    echo "$host is unreachable"

  fi

done
```

This script uses fping to check the connectivity to a list of hosts and reports whether each one is reachable or not.

Example: Monitoring a Web Server with nc

Bash

```bash
#!/bin/bash

host="www.example.com"

port="80"

while true; do

  if nc -zv $host $port > /dev/null 2>&1; then

    echo "$(date) - $host:$port is open"

  else

    echo "$(date) - $host:$port is closed"

  fi

  sleep 60  # Check every minute

done
```

This script continuously checks if a specific port (port 80 in this case) is open on a web server.

Real-World Examples

- Monitoring Network Devices: You can use ping to monitor the availability of critical network devices like routers, switches, and firewalls.
- Website Monitoring: You can use fping or nc to monitor the availability of your websites or web applications, ensuring that they are always accessible to users.

- VPN Connectivity: You can check the connectivity to your VPN server to ensure that the VPN tunnel is established and working correctly.[10]
- Cloud Instance Monitoring: You can monitor the connectivity to your cloud instances to ensure that they are reachable and responding.

Exercises

1. Use ping to check the connectivity to different hosts on your network and on the internet.
2. Write a Bash script that uses fping to check the connectivity to a list of hosts and saves the results to a file.
3. Use nc to check if specific ports (e.g., 22 for SSH, 443 for HTTPS) are open on a remote server.
4. Write a Bash script that continuously monitors the connectivity to a critical server and sends an email alert if the server becomes unreachable.

7.3 Monitoring Network Performance

Monitoring network performance goes beyond simply checking if devices are reachable. It's like measuring the vital signs of your network – checking its blood pressure (latency), heart rate (packet loss), and breathing (jitter). By keeping a close eye on these metrics, you can ensure your network is running at its best and identify potential problems before they impact users or applications.

Why Monitor Network Performance?

- Optimize User Experience: Network performance directly impacts the experience of users on your network.[1] Slow response times, dropped connections, and inconsistent performance can frustrate users and hinder productivity.[2]

- Identify Bottlenecks: Performance monitoring helps you pinpoint bottlenecks in your network, such as overloaded links, congested routers, or misconfigured devices.[3]
- Ensure Application Performance: Many applications, especially real-time applications like video conferencing and online gaming, are sensitive to network performance.[4] Monitoring helps ensure these applications run smoothly.[5]
- Plan for Capacity: By tracking performance trends over time, you can predict future needs and plan for upgrades or expansions to your network infrastructure.[6]
- Troubleshooting: When network problems occur, performance data is crucial for diagnosing the root cause and finding solutions.[7]

Key Network Performance Metrics

- Latency: This measures the time it takes for a data packet to travel from the source to the destination and back.[8] It's usually measured in milliseconds (ms).[9] High latency can cause slow response times and delays in applications.[10]
- Packet Loss: This measures the percentage of data packets that are lost in transit.[11] Packet loss can result in dropped connections, corrupted data, and poor application performance.[12]
- Jitter: This measures the variation in latency between packets. High jitter can cause inconsistent performance and disruptions in real-time applications.[13]
- Bandwidth: While we discussed bandwidth monitoring in detail earlier, it's also an important performance metric. Insufficient bandwidth can lead to congestion and slowdowns.[14]

Tools for Monitoring Network Performance

Bash provides access to various tools for monitoring network performance:

- **ping:** While primarily used for connectivity checks, ping also provides valuable information about latency (round-trip time) and packet loss.

Bash

```
ping -c 4 www.google.com
```

- mtr **(My Traceroute):** This tool combines the functionality of ping and traceroute. It sends a stream of packets to a destination host and provides continuous measurements of latency and packet loss for each hop along the path. This helps you identify bottlenecks and visualize network performance across multiple hops.[15]

Bash

mtr www.example.com

- **iperf:** This tool is specifically designed for measuring the bandwidth and quality of a network connection.[16] It can generate TCP and UDP traffic to test the throughput and latency of your network.[17]

Bash

```
iperf -c 192.168.1.10 -t 30  # Send TCP traffic
to 192.168.1.10 for 30 seconds
```

Scripting Performance Monitoring with Bash

You can use these tools in your Bash scripts to automate performance monitoring and create custom monitoring solutions.

Example: Monitoring Latency with ping

Bash

```bash
#!/bin/bash

host="www.example.com"

threshold="100"  # Latency threshold in
milliseconds

while true; do

  latency=$(ping -c 4 $host | tail -1 | awk
'{print $4}' | cut -d '/' -f 2)

  if (( latency > threshold )); then

    echo "Warning: High latency to $host:
$latency ms"

  fi

  sleep 60  # Check every minute

done
```

This script continuously pings a host and checks if the average latency exceeds a defined threshold. If it does, it prints a warning message.

Example: Logging Performance Data with mtr

Bash

```bash
#!/bin/bash

host="www.google.com"

logfile="mtr_log.txt"
```

```
# Run mtr and capture the report

mtr --report --report-cycles 30 $host > $logfile

# Analyze the log file for performance issues

# ...
```

This script uses mtr to generate a performance report with 30 cycles (samples) and saves it to a file. You can then analyze this file for patterns of high latency or packet loss.[18]

Real-World Examples

- Monitoring VoIP Quality: You can use ping or mtr to monitor the latency and jitter of your network connection, which are critical factors for VoIP (Voice over IP) call quality.
- Troubleshooting VPN Performance: If you're experiencing slow performance with your VPN connection, you can use mtr to identify which hop along the VPN tunnel is causing the bottleneck.
- Testing Network Upgrades: After upgrading your network infrastructure (e.g., new router, faster internet connection), you can use iperf to measure the performance improvement and ensure that you're getting the expected bandwidth.

Exercises

1. Use ping to monitor the latency to different websites and compare the results.
2. Use mtr to monitor the network performance to a remote host and identify any hops with high latency or packet loss.
3. Use iperf to measure the bandwidth between two computers on your network.
4. Write a Bash script that continuously monitors the latency to a critical server and sends an email alert if the latency exceeds a certain threshold.

By mastering network performance monitoring with Bash, you gain the ability to proactively identify and address performance issues, optimize your network infrastructure, and ensure a smooth and efficient user experience.

7.4 Detecting Network Anomalies

Detecting network anomalies is like having a security system for your network that can identify unusual or suspicious activity. It's about going beyond routine monitoring and looking for those subtle signs that something might be amiss. With Bash and the right tools, you can automate the detection of these anomalies and proactively protect your network from potential threats or problems.

Why Detect Network Anomalies?

- Security: Network anomalies can often be indicators of malicious activity, such as port scans, denial-of-service attacks, or attempts to exploit vulnerabilities. Detecting these anomalies early on can help you prevent or mitigate security breaches.
- Troubleshooting: Unusual network behavior can also be a sign of network problems, such as misconfigured devices, faulty hardware, or performance bottlenecks. Anomaly detection can help you identify and address these issues before they cause major disruptions.
- Network Optimization: By analyzing network traffic patterns and identifying anomalies, you can gain insights into how your network is being used and optimize its performance.
- Proactive Management: Anomaly detection allows you to move from reactive to proactive network management, addressing potential problems before they impact users or applications.

Types of Network Anomalies

Network anomalies can take many forms, including:

- Unusual Traffic Spikes: Sudden increases in network traffic, especially on specific ports or protocols, can indicate malicious activity like DDoS attacks or data exfiltration.
- Suspicious Connection Attempts: Repeated failed login attempts, port scans, or connections from known malicious IP addresses can be signs of unauthorized access attempts.
- Unexpected Network Behavior: Changes in network performance, unusual traffic patterns, or unexpected device behavior can indicate network misconfigurations or hardware problems.

Tools for Anomaly Detection

Bash provides access to various tools for detecting network anomalies:

- tcpdump: This powerful tool allows you to capture and analyze network traffic. You can use it to identify unusual patterns, such as high volumes of traffic on specific ports, or to detect suspicious packets based on their content.
- psad (Port Scan Attack Detection): This tool analyzes iptables log messages to detect port scans and other suspicious network activity. It can alert you to potential reconnaissance attempts by attackers.
- fail2ban: This tool monitors log files (like SSH logs) and automatically blocks IP addresses that exhibit malicious behavior, such as repeated failed login attempts. It helps to prevent brute-force attacks and other unauthorized access attempts.
- Intrusion Detection/Prevention Systems (IDS/IPS): These systems monitor network traffic for suspicious activity and can either alert you to potential threats (IDS) or actively block them (IPS).

Scripting Anomaly Detection with Bash

You can use these tools in combination with Bash scripts to automate network anomaly detection.

Example: Analyzing tcpdump Output

```bash
Bash

#!/bin/bash

interface="eth0"

threshold="1000"  # Threshold for packets per
second

# Capture traffic for 1 minute

sudo tcpdump -i $interface -w traffic.pcap -G 60

# Analyze the captured traffic (example: count
packets per second)

packets_per_second=$(tcpdump -r traffic.pcap | wc
-l) / 60

if (( packets_per_second > threshold )); then

  echo "Warning: High traffic volume detected:
$packets_per_second packets per second"

fi
```

This script captures network traffic using tcpdump, calculates the average packets per second, and checks if it exceeds a defined threshold.

Example: Enhancing fail2ban with Bash

Bash

```bash
#!/bin/bash

# Get the list of banned IPs from fail2ban

banned_ips=$(fail2ban-client status sshd | grep
"Banned IP list" | awk '{print $4}')

# Perform actions on the banned IPs (e.g.,
reverse DNS lookup, email alerts)

for ip in $banned_ips; do

  hostname=$(dig -x $ip +short)

  echo "Banned IP: $ip ($hostname)"

done
```

This script retrieves the list of banned IP addresses from fail2ban and performs a reverse DNS lookup on each IP to get the hostname.

Real-World Examples

- Detecting DDoS Attacks: You can use tcpdump or an IDS/IPS to monitor for sudden spikes in network traffic that might indicate a DDoS attack.
- Identifying Compromised Systems: Unusual outgoing connections or high volumes of traffic from a specific device might indicate that the device has been compromised by malware.
- Monitoring for Port Scans: You can use psad to detect port scans, which are often a precursor to more serious attacks.

Exercises

1. Use tcpdump to capture network traffic on your system and analyze it for any unusual patterns or suspicious activity.
2. Install psad and configure it to monitor your firewall logs for port scans.
3. Write a Bash script that parses fail2ban log files and sends an email alert when an IP address is banned.
4. Research different types of network anomalies and how to detect them using various tools and techniques.

7.5 Generating Alerts

Generating alerts, a crucial aspect of network monitoring. It's not enough to just monitor your network; you need a way to be notified when something goes wrong or when an unusual event occurs. Think of it like a smoke detector in your house – it's constantly monitoring for smoke, but it's the alarm that actually wakes you up and prompts you to take action. Similarly, network alerts notify you of potential problems or security threats, allowing you to respond quickly and prevent or mitigate damage.

Why Generate Alerts?

- Timely Response: Alerts enable you to respond to network issues in a timely manner, minimizing downtime and preventing further damage.
- Proactive Management: Alerts help you move from reactive to proactive network management, addressing potential problems before they escalate and impact users or applications.
- Increased Awareness: Alerts keep you informed about the state of your network, even when you're not actively monitoring it.

- Improved Security: Alerts can notify you of security breaches or suspicious activity, allowing you to take immediate action to protect your network.
- Automation: You can integrate alerts with automated response mechanisms to trigger actions like blocking IP addresses, restarting services, or escalating the issue to a human operator.

Alerting Methods

There are various ways to generate alerts from your Bash scripts:

- Email: Email is a common and reliable method for sending alerts. You can use the mail command or a mail server to send email notifications to your inbox.
- SMS: For urgent alerts, you can use SMS (Short Message Service) to send notifications directly to your phone. You can use services like Twilio or Nexmo to send SMS messages from your scripts.
- Slack/Other Messaging Platforms: You can integrate your scripts with messaging platforms like Slack, Microsoft Teams, or Discord to send alerts to specific channels or users. This is particularly useful for team collaboration and incident response.
- Push Notifications: You can use push notification services like Pushover or Pushbullet to send alerts to your mobile devices or desktop computers.
- Syslog: You can send alerts to your system log (syslog) for centralized logging and analysis.

Scripting Alerts with Bash

Let's see how you can use Bash to generate alerts using different methods:

Example: Sending an Email Alert

Bash

```bash
#!/bin/bash

recipient="your_email@example.com"

subject="Network Alert"

message="High latency detected on
www.example.com"

echo "$message" | mail -s "$subject" "$recipient"
```

This script sends a simple email alert with the specified subject and message.

Example: Sending an SMS Alert with Twilio

Bash

```bash
#!/bin/bash

# Twilio account credentials

account_sid="ACxxxxxxxxxxxxxxxxxxxxxxxxxxxxxxxx"  # Replace with your Account SID

auth_token="your_auth_token"                      # Replace with your Auth Token

# Phone numbers

from_number="+1234567890"  # Replace with your Twilio phone number

to_number="+11234567890"    # Replace with your phone number
```

```
message="Critical server is down!"

# Send the SMS alert

curl -X POST
https://api.twilio.com/2010-04-01/Accounts/$accou
nt_sid/Messages.json \

    --data-urlencode "From=$from_number" \

    --data-urlencode "To=$to_number" \

    --data-urlencode "Body=$message" \

    -u $account_sid:$auth_token
```

This script uses the Twilio API to send an SMS alert. You'll need to create a Twilio account and obtain the necessary credentials.

Example: Sending a Slack Alert

Bash

```
#!/bin/bash

webhook_url="https://hooks.slack.com/services/TXX
XXXXX/BXXXXXXXX/xxxxxxxxxxxxx"   # Replace with
your Slack webhook URL

message="Server is back online!"

# Send the Slack alert

curl -X POST -H 'Content-type: application/json'
--data '{"text":"'$message'"}' $webhook_url
```

This script sends a message to a Slack channel using a webhook URL. You'll need to create a webhook integration in your Slack workspace.

Real-World Examples

- Server Monitoring: You can configure alerts to notify you when a server goes down, experiences high CPU usage, or runs out of disk space.
- Security Alerts: You can set up alerts for suspicious login attempts, port scans, or other security-related events.
- Network Performance Alerts: You can generate alerts when network latency exceeds a certain threshold, packet loss increases, or bandwidth usage reaches a critical level.
- Application Monitoring: You can monitor your applications and generate alerts for errors, performance degradation, or unusual behavior.

Exercises

1. Write a Bash script that sends an email alert when a specific process is not running.
2. Set up a Twilio account and write a Bash script that sends an SMS alert when your internet connection goes down.
3. Create a Slack webhook integration and write a Bash script that sends a message to a Slack channel when a critical server is restarted.
4. Research other alerting methods (Pushover, Pushbullet, Syslog) and experiment with integrating them into your Bash scripts.

By mastering alert generation with Bash, you can ensure that you're always informed about the state of your network and can respond quickly to any issues that arise.

Chapter 8: Log Analysis and Reporting

Think of network logs as the diary of your network. They contain a wealth of information about what's happening on your network, from routine events to security incidents and performance issues. With Bash, you can become a network detective, sifting through these logs, extracting valuable insights, and generating reports that help you understand and manage your network more effectively.

8.1 Parsing Network Logs

Let's talk about parsing network logs, an essential skill for any network administrator or security professional. Think of network logs as the chronicles of your network, recording everything that happens – from routine events like user logins and website visits to critical security incidents and performance issues. Parsing these logs is like deciphering a secret code, extracting meaningful information from raw data and turning it into actionable insights.

Why Parse Network Logs?

- Troubleshooting: When something goes wrong on your network, logs are often the first place you turn to for clues. Parsing logs helps you identify the source of problems, track down errors, and understand the sequence of events that led to an issue.[1]
- Security Analysis: Logs can reveal suspicious activity, such as unauthorized access attempts, malware infections, or data breaches.[2] Parsing security logs helps you identify and respond to security threats.[3]
- Performance Optimization: Logs can contain valuable performance data, such as network latency, bandwidth usage, and server response times.[4] Parsing these logs can

help you identify bottlenecks and optimize network performance.[5]

- Compliance and Auditing: Many organizations have regulatory requirements to maintain logs and demonstrate compliance with security standards.[6] Parsing logs helps you extract the necessary information for audits and reports.[7]
- Understanding Network Behavior: By analyzing log data, you can gain a deeper understanding of how your network is being used, identify trends, and predict future needs.

Tools for Parsing Network Logs

Bash provides a powerful toolkit for parsing network logs:

- grep: This command is your go-to tool for searching for specific patterns in text files.[8] You can use it to find log entries that contain certain keywords, IP addresses, error messages, or any other text string.

Bash

```
grep "failed login" /var/log/auth.log
```

This command searches the authentication log file (/var/log/auth.log) for lines containing the phrase "failed login."

- awk: This versatile tool is like a Swiss Army knife for text processing.[9] It allows you to extract specific fields from structured data, perform calculations, and manipulate text in various ways.

Bash

```
awk '{print $1, $4}' access.log
```

This command extracts the first and fourth fields (typically the IP address and timestamp) from each line of a web server access log file (access.log).

- **cut:** This command is used to extract specific columns or fields from text data.[10] It's simpler than awk but can be useful for basic parsing tasks.

Bash

```
cut -d ',' -f 2,5 data.csv
```

This command extracts the second and fifth fields from a comma-separated value (CSV) file (data.csv).

- **sed:** This stream editor allows you to perform text transformations, such as replacing text, deleting lines, or inserting new content.[11] It's useful for cleaning up log files or reformatting data before further analysis.

Bash

```
sed 's/192.168.1.10/localhost/g' logfile.txt
```

This command replaces all occurrences of the IP address "192.168.1.10" with "localhost" in the logfile.txt file.

Combining Tools for Advanced Parsing

You can combine these tools using pipes (|) to create powerful parsing pipelines.

Example: Extracting Error Messages and Timestamps

Bash

```
grep "error" /var/log/syslog | awk '{print $1 " "
$2 " " $3 ": " $8}'
```

This command first searches the system log for lines containing "error" and then uses awk to extract the date, time, and the error message itself.

Real-World Examples

- Analyzing Web Server Logs: You can use awk to extract information from web server access logs, such as the most visited pages, the top referrers, or the number of requests from each IP address.
- Identifying Security Breaches: You can use grep to search security logs for suspicious activity, such as failed login attempts, unauthorized access to files, or malware signatures.
- Troubleshooting Network Connectivity: You can use awk and grep to analyze network logs and identify the source of connectivity problems, such as dropped packets, routing errors, or DNS resolution failures.

Exercises

1. Use grep to search a log file for a specific IP address.
2. Use awk to extract the username and login time from an authentication log file.
3. Write a Bash script that parses a firewall log and extracts all the blocked IP addresses.
4. Use sed to remove all lines containing a specific keyword from a log file.

By mastering log parsing with Bash, you gain the ability to extract valuable information from your network logs, identify trends, troubleshoot problems, and enhance your network security.

8.2 Extracting Key Information

Let's extract key information from network logs. After you've parsed the logs and filtered out the noise, you're left with the important stuff – the nuggets of knowledge that can help you understand your network, troubleshoot problems, and enhance security. It's like panning for gold – you sift through a lot of dirt and gravel to find those precious nuggets.

Why Extract Key Information?

- Focus on what matters: Raw log files can be overwhelming. Extracting key information helps you focus on the data that is most relevant to your needs, whether it's error messages, IP addresses, performance metrics, or security events.
- Make data actionable: Extracted information can be used to generate reports, create alerts, or trigger automated responses.
- Gain insights: By analyzing extracted data, you can identify trends, patterns, and anomalies that might not be obvious from raw logs.
- Improve decision-making: Key information provides the basis for informed decision-making about network management, security, and optimization.

Identifying Key Information

The key information you need to extract depends on your specific goals and the type of logs you're analyzing. Here are some common examples:

- Error Messages: Error messages provide valuable clues for troubleshooting problems. You'll want to extract the error message itself, the timestamp, and any associated context (such as the source IP address or the affected service).

- IP Addresses: IP addresses can help you identify the source of network traffic, track down malicious actors, or analyze communication patterns.
- Usernames and Authentication Events: Extracting usernames and authentication events (logins, logouts, failed attempts) is crucial for security auditing and user activity tracking.
- Timestamps: Timestamps provide context for events and help you understand the sequence of events leading up to a problem or security incident.
- Performance Metrics: Extract performance data like latency, packet loss, bandwidth usage, and CPU utilization to monitor network health and identify bottlenecks.

Tools and Techniques for Extraction

You can use the same tools we discussed in the previous section (grep, awk, cut, sed) to extract key information.

Example: Extracting SSH Login Attempts from auth.log

Bash

```
#!/bin/bash

logfile="/var/log/auth.log"

# Extract SSH login attempts (successful and failed)

grep "sshd" $logfile | awk '{print $1 " " $2 " " $3 " " $9 " " $11}'
```

This script extracts the date, time, user, IP address, and login status from SSH-related log entries in the auth.log file.

Example: Extracting Error Messages from a Web Server Log

Bash

```bash
#!/bin/bash

logfile="/var/log/apache2/error.log"

# Extract error messages and their timestamps

grep "\[error\]" $logfile | awk '{print $1 " " $2 " " $3 ": " $8}'
```

This script extracts the date, time, and error message from lines containing "[error]" in an Apache error log.

Example: Extracting Top Bandwidth Consumers from iftop Output

Bash

```bash
#!/bin/bash

interface="eth0"

duration="10"   # Monitor for 10 seconds

# Capture iftop output

iftop -i $interface -t -s $duration > iftop_output.txt

# Extract the top 5 bandwidth consumers (source
and destination IP addresses)

grep "=>" iftop_output.txt | head -5 | awk '{print $1, $3}'
```

This script captures iftop output and extracts the source and destination IP addresses of the top 5 bandwidth consumers.

Real-World Examples

- Security Incident Response: Extracting key information from security logs can help you quickly identify the source of an attack, the affected systems, and the extent of the damage.
- Performance Troubleshooting: Extracting performance metrics from logs can help you pinpoint bottlenecks, identify slow applications, or diagnose network connectivity issues.
- User Activity Monitoring: Extracting user login and activity data can help you track user behavior, identify suspicious activity, or generate reports on user access patterns.

Exercises

1. Write a Bash script that extracts all the IP addresses that accessed a specific file on your web server from the access log.
2. Write a Bash script that extracts all the failed login attempts from your system's authentication log and saves them to a separate file.
3. Analyze a network performance log and extract the average latency and packet loss for a specific connection.
4. Write a Bash script that extracts the top 10 most frequent error messages from a log file.

8.3 Generating Reports

Generating reports from your network log analysis after you've parsed those logs and extracted the key information, you need a way to present your findings in a clear and organized manner. Think of it like writing a detective's report – you need to summarize your investigation, present the evidence, and draw conclusions that others can understand and act upon.

Why Generate Reports?

- Communication: Reports help you communicate your findings to others, whether it's your team, your manager, or security auditors.
- Documentation: Reports provide a record of your analysis, which can be useful for tracking trends, troubleshooting recurring problems, or demonstrating compliance with security regulations.
- Decision-Making: Well-structured reports can help you make informed decisions about network management, security, and optimization.
- Visualization: Reports can include visualizations like graphs and charts that make it easier to understand complex data and identify patterns.
- Automation: You can automate the generation of reports, saving time and effort while ensuring consistent reporting formats.

Report Formats

There are various formats you can use for your network reports:

- Plain Text Reports: These are the simplest type of report, consisting of plain text with basic formatting. They are easy to generate and can be viewed in any text editor.
- CSV/TSV Reports: Comma-separated value (CSV) or tab-separated value (TSV) reports are structured data formats that can be easily imported into spreadsheets or other data analysis tools. This allows for further analysis, sorting, and visualization of the data.
- HTML Reports: HTML reports provide a more visually appealing and interactive way to present your findings. You

can use HTML to create tables, charts, and other visual elements that make the report easier to understand.

- PDF Reports: PDF (Portable Document Format) reports are widely used for sharing and archiving documents. They preserve the formatting of the report and can be easily viewed and printed on different platforms.

Tools for Generating Reports

Bash provides several tools for generating reports:

- awk: awk is a versatile tool that can be used to format and generate reports in various formats, including plain text, CSV, and TSV.
- printf: This command provides more precise formatting options for generating reports, allowing you to control the alignment, spacing, and precision of your output.
- Specialized Reporting Tools: You can use tools like gnuplot or reportlab (a Python library) to generate graphs, charts, and other visual elements in your reports.

Example: Generating a Simple Text Report

Bash

```bash
#!/bin/bash

logfile="/var/log/apache2/access.log"

# Extract the top 10 most visited pages

echo "Top 10 most visited pages:"

awk '{print $7}' $logfile | sort | uniq -c | sort -rn | head -10
```

This script extracts the requested URLs from an Apache access log, counts their occurrences, and displays the top 10 most visited pages in a simple text format.

Example: Generating a CSV Report

Bash

```
#!/bin/bash

logfile="/var/log/auth.log"

# Extract SSH login attempts and save to a CSV
file

echo "Date,Time,User,IP Address,Status" >
ssh_logins.csv

grep "sshd" $logfile | awk '{print $1 "," $2 ","
$3 "," $9 "," $11}' >> ssh_logins.csv
```

This script extracts SSH login attempts from the authentication log and saves them to a CSV file with appropriate headers.

Real-World Examples

- Security Audit Reports: You can generate reports that summarize security events, such as failed login attempts, suspicious network activity, or detected malware.
- Network Performance Reports: You can generate reports that show network latency, packet loss, bandwidth usage, and other performance metrics over time.
- Website Traffic Reports: You can analyze web server logs to generate reports on website traffic, including the number of visitors, most popular pages, and referrers.
- Compliance Reports: You can generate reports that demonstrate compliance with security regulations or internal policies.

Exercises

1. Write a Bash script that analyzes a firewall log and generates a report of the blocked IP addresses, including the number of times each IP was blocked.
2. Write a Bash script that generates a CSV report of network performance data, including timestamps, latency, and packet loss.
3. Research the printf command and learn how to use it for advanced formatting in your reports.
4. Explore reporting tools like gnuplot or reportlab and learn how to generate graphs and charts in your reports.

8.4 Visualizing Network Data

Visualizing network data is a powerful way to gain insights from your network logs and monitoring tools. You see, while raw numbers and text logs can be informative, they can also be overwhelming. Visualizing this data – turning it into graphs, charts, and dashboards – can make it much easier to understand patterns, trends, and anomalies that might be hidden in the raw data. Think of it like looking at a map instead of a list of street addresses – the map gives you a much clearer picture of where things are and how they relate to each other.

Why Visualize Network Data?

- Identify Patterns and Trends: Visualizations can reveal patterns and trends in your network traffic that might not be obvious from raw data. This can help you understand how your network is being used, identify peak usage times, and predict future needs.
- Detect Anomalies: Visualizations can make it easier to spot anomalies, such as sudden spikes in traffic, unusual connection patterns, or performance deviations. This can

help you identify potential problems or security threats early on.

- Communicate Effectively: Visualizations are a powerful way to communicate your findings to others. A well-designed graph or chart can convey complex information quickly and effectively, making it easier for others to understand your analysis.
- Monitor Network Health: Visualizations can be used to create dashboards that provide a real-time view of your network's health, allowing you to monitor key metrics and identify potential issues at a glance.
- Gain Deeper Insights: By exploring data visually, you can often gain deeper insights and uncover hidden relationships that might not be apparent from raw data.

Tools for Visualizing Network Data

Bash, combined with other tools, provides several options for visualizing network data:

- gnuplot: This command-line tool is a versatile plotting utility that can generate a wide variety of graphs, including line graphs, bar charts, scatter plots, and more. It's a powerful tool for creating visualizations from data in text files or from the output of other commands.
- matplotlib (with Python): If you're comfortable with Python, the matplotlib library provides a comprehensive set of plotting functions for creating high-quality visualizations. You can use it to generate various types of graphs and customize their appearance to meet your needs.
- Web-based Dashboards: Tools like Grafana and Kibana provide powerful platforms for creating interactive web-based dashboards. These dashboards can display data from various sources, including network logs, monitoring tools, and databases. They allow you to create dynamic visualizations, set up alerts, and explore your data in real-time.

Example: Generating a Line Graph with gnuplot

Bash

```bash
#!/bin/bash

datafile="bandwidth_data.txt"  # Assume this file
contains timestamps and bandwidth values

# Generate a line graph of bandwidth usage over
time

gnuplot << EOF

set xdata time

set timefmt "%Y-%m-%d %H:%M:%S"

set format x "%Y-%m-%d"

set xlabel "Date"

set ylabel "Bandwidth (Mbps)"

plot "$datafile" using 1:2 with lines title
"Bandwidth Usage"

EOF
```

This script uses gnuplot to generate a line graph from a data file containing timestamps and bandwidth values. It sets the x-axis to display time, formats the date, and plots the data as a line graph.

Example: Creating a Bar Chart with matplotlib (Python)

Python

```python
import matplotlib.pyplot as plt

# Sample data (replace with your actual data)
```

```
labels = ['Host A', 'Host B', 'Host C']

bandwidth = [100, 250, 180]

# Create the bar chart

plt.bar(labels, bandwidth)

plt.xlabel("Hosts")

plt.ylabel("Bandwidth (Mbps)")

plt.title("Bandwidth Usage by Host")

plt.show()
```

This Python script uses matplotlib to create a bar chart showing bandwidth usage by different hosts.

Real-World Examples

- Network Traffic Analysis: Visualize network traffic patterns over time to identify peak hours, bandwidth bottlenecks, and unusual activity.
- Security Monitoring: Create dashboards that display security events, such as intrusion attempts, malware detections, and suspicious logins.
- Performance Monitoring: Visualize performance metrics like latency, packet loss, and jitter to identify trends and potential problems.
- Capacity Planning: Use historical data to visualize network growth and predict future capacity needs.

Exercises

1. Install gnuplot and use it to create a simple line graph from a data file.
2. If you have Python installed, install matplotlib and use it to create a bar chart or scatter plot from sample data.

3. Research Grafana or Kibana and explore their features for creating network dashboards.
4. Think about how you could use visualizations to present the findings from your network log analysis or monitoring scripts.

By mastering network data visualization with Bash and other tools, you can unlock the power of visual analysis, gain deeper insights into your network behavior, and communicate your findings more effectively. This is a valuable skill for any network administrator who wants to understand and manage their network in a more intuitive and impactful way.

Chapter 9: Troubleshooting Network Connectivity

Troubleshooting network connectivity is one of the most critical skills for any network administrator. Think of it like being a network doctor – you need to diagnose the problem, identify the root cause, and prescribe the right solution to get your network back to health. With Bash and the right tools, you can become a network detective, investigating connectivity issues, pinpointing bottlenecks, and even automating some of the troubleshooting process.

9.1 Diagnosing Network Problems

Think of yourself as a network detective, faced with a connectivity puzzle. Your mission is to gather clues, analyze the evidence, and pinpoint the culprit causing the network disruption. With a systematic approach and the right tools, you can effectively diagnose network problems and restore connectivity.

Importance of Diagnosis

Before jumping into solutions, it's essential to understand *why* diagnosing network problems is so important:

- Targeted Solutions: Accurate diagnosis leads to targeted solutions, saving you time and effort. Instead of randomly trying different fixes, you can focus on addressing the root cause of the problem.
- Minimizing Downtime: Quick diagnosis helps minimize network downtime, which is critical for businesses and organizations that rely on network connectivity for their operations.

- Preventing Recurrence: By understanding the underlying cause of a network problem, you can take steps to prevent it from happening again.
- Learning and Improvement: Every troubleshooting experience is a learning opportunity. By carefully diagnosing problems, you gain a deeper understanding of your network and improve your troubleshooting skills.

Common Network Connectivity Symptoms

Network problems can manifest in various ways. Here are some common symptoms:

- Complete Network Outage: No devices can connect to the network. This could indicate a problem with the network infrastructure (e.g., a faulty router or switch), a widespread internet outage, or a misconfiguration in core network devices.
- Intermittent Connectivity: The network connection drops in and out, causing disruptions to applications and services. This could be due to wireless interference, loose cables, faulty network cards, or intermittent problems with your internet service provider (ISP).
- Slow Network Performance: The network feels sluggish, websites load slowly, and applications are unresponsive. This could be caused by network congestion, bandwidth limitations, overloaded servers, or problems with specific applications.
- Inability to Reach Specific Resources: You can connect to the network but can't access certain websites, servers, or online services. This could indicate DNS resolution problems, firewall restrictions, or issues with the remote resource itself.

A Systematic Approach to Diagnosis

1. Gather Information: Start by gathering as much information as possible about the problem. Talk to users who are experiencing the issue, check system logs for error messages, and review network monitoring data to identify any unusual patterns or trends.

2. Check the Basics: Before diving into complex troubleshooting, check the basics:
   - Physical Connections: Ensure all network cables are securely connected and there's no visible damage.
   - Wireless Signal Strength: If using Wi-Fi, check the signal strength and ensure you're connected to the correct network.
   - Device Configuration: Verify the device's network settings, including the IP address, subnet mask, and default gateway. Make sure the network interface is enabled.

3. Isolate the Problem: Try to isolate the problem to a specific device, network segment, or application. This will help you narrow down the possible causes. For example:
   - Is the problem affecting all devices or just one?
   - Is the problem specific to a particular website or application?
   - Does the problem occur only at certain times of the day?

4. Utilize Diagnostic Tools: Bash provides access to powerful diagnostic tools that can help you pinpoint the source of the problem:
   - ping: Use ping to test basic connectivity to a remote host. This will tell you if the host is reachable and provide information about latency and packet loss.
   - traceroute: Use traceroute to trace the path that packets take to reach a destination. This can help you identify network bottlenecks or connectivity issues along the route.

- nslookup **or** dig**:** Use these tools to check DNS resolution. Make sure that domain names are correctly resolving to IP addresses.
- tcpdump**:** This tool allows you to capture and analyze network traffic. It can be useful for identifying unusual patterns, dropped packets, or other network anomalies.
5. Analyze the Results: Carefully analyze the output of the diagnostic tools to understand what's happening on the network. Look for patterns of high latency, packet loss, or error messages that might indicate the source of the problem.
6. Formulate a Hypothesis: Based on your analysis, formulate a hypothesis about the cause of the problem. This will guide your further investigation and help you choose the appropriate solution.
7. Test Your Hypothesis: Test your hypothesis by making changes to your network configuration, updating drivers, or trying alternative solutions. Monitor the results to see if the problem is resolved.
8. Document Your Findings: Document the steps you took, the results of your analysis, and the solution you implemented. This will be valuable for future troubleshooting or for sharing your knowledge with others.

Real-World Examples

- Troubleshooting a Website Outage: If you can't access a website, you might use ping to check if the web server is reachable. If the ping fails, you could use traceroute to see where the connection is failing. If the traceroute shows that the problem is with your ISP's network, you might need to contact them for support.
- Diagnosing Slow Network Performance: If your network is slow, you might use iperf to measure the bandwidth of your internet connection. If the bandwidth is lower than

expected, you might need to contact your ISP or upgrade your internet plan. You could also use iftop to identify any devices or applications that are consuming excessive bandwidth.

- Troubleshooting DNS Problems: If you can't access websites by name but can access them by IP address, you might use nslookup or dig to check if DNS resolution is working correctly. If you're not getting the correct IP address, you might need to change your DNS server settings.

Exercises

1. Use ping and traceroute to diagnose a connectivity problem to a website or server of your choice.
2. Use mtr to identify any network bottlenecks between your computer and a remote host.
3. Practice analyzing the output of tcpdump to identify unusual network traffic patterns.
4. Research common network error messages and learn how to interpret them.

By mastering the art of diagnosing network problems, you become a more effective network administrator, capable of quickly identifying and resolving connectivity issues

9.2 Identifying Bottlenecks

Let's talk about identifying network bottlenecks, a crucial skill for optimizing network performance. Think of a bottleneck as a constriction in a water pipe – it restricts the flow of water, reducing the overall output. Similarly, a network bottleneck restricts the flow of data, causing slowdowns, delays, and frustrating performance issues.

Why Identify Bottlenecks?

- Improve Performance: By identifying and addressing bottlenecks, you can significantly improve the overall performance of your network. This means faster downloads, smoother streaming, and more responsive applications.
- Optimize Resource Utilization: Bottlenecks often indicate that resources are not being used efficiently. Identifying them allows you to redistribute resources or upgrade specific components to improve overall network efficiency.
- Reduce Costs: In some cases, bottlenecks can lead to unnecessary costs, such as increased bandwidth usage or the need for more powerful hardware. Addressing bottlenecks can help you optimize your network infrastructure and reduce these costs.
- Enhance User Experience: Network bottlenecks can negatively impact the user experience, causing frustration and hindering productivity. Identifying and resolving bottlenecks can lead to a more satisfying and productive experience for users.

Where Bottlenecks Occur

Network bottlenecks can occur at various points in your network infrastructure:

- Network Interfaces: A slow or overloaded network interface card (NIC) can limit the amount of data that can be transmitted or received, creating a bottleneck. This is often the case with older or low-quality NICs.
- Network Links: A slow or congested network link, such as a shared internet connection or a low-bandwidth WAN link, can restrict the overall throughput of your network.
- Routers and Switches: Overloaded routers or switches can become bottlenecks, especially if they are not configured to handle the volume of traffic on your network.

- Servers and Applications: A server that is overloaded or an application that consumes excessive bandwidth can create a bottleneck, affecting the performance of other applications and services on the network.
- Firewalls: A misconfigured or overloaded firewall can also become a bottleneck, especially if it performs deep packet inspection or other resource-intensive operations.
- Client Devices: In some cases, the bottleneck might be on the client device itself, such as a slow CPU, limited memory, or a congested wireless connection.

Tools for Identifying Bottlenecks

- **mtr** (My Traceroute): This tool is invaluable for identifying bottlenecks along a network path. It combines the functionality of ping and traceroute, providing continuous measurements of latency and packet loss for each hop between your computer and a destination host. By analyzing the mtr output, you can pinpoint which hop is experiencing high latency or packet loss, indicating a potential bottleneck.
- iperf: This tool is specifically designed for measuring the bandwidth and quality of a network connection. You can use it to test the throughput between two points on your network and identify any links or devices that are limiting the transfer speed.
- Network Monitoring Tools: Comprehensive network monitoring tools like Nagios, Zabbix, or Datadog can monitor various network devices and services for performance issues. They can collect metrics like CPU utilization, memory usage, interface statistics, and bandwidth consumption, helping you identify potential bottlenecks.
- Bandwidth Monitoring Tools: Tools like vnstat, iftop, and bmon (discussed earlier) can help you identify which

applications or devices are consuming the most bandwidth, which might be contributing to a bottleneck.

Analyzing Data to Pinpoint Bottlenecks

Identifying bottlenecks often involves analyzing data from these tools and looking for patterns or anomalies:

- High Latency: Consistently high latency on a specific hop in an mtr report might indicate a congested router or a slow link.
- Packet Loss: Packet loss on a specific hop can also indicate congestion or a problem with that link or device.
- Low Bandwidth: If iperf reports lower bandwidth than expected, it might indicate a bottleneck on the link or at one of the endpoints.
- High Resource Utilization: If your monitoring tools show high CPU utilization, memory usage, or interface load on a specific device, it might be a bottleneck.

Real-World Examples

- Troubleshooting Slow Internet: If your internet connection feels slow, you can use mtr to trace the route to a website and identify if the bottleneck is within your home network, your ISP's network, or somewhere in between.
- Optimizing Application Performance: If a specific application is performing poorly, you can use iperf to test the bandwidth between the client and the server and identify any bottlenecks along the path. You can also monitor the server's resource usage to see if it's overloaded.
- Identifying Network Congestion: If your network is experiencing congestion during peak hours, you can use bandwidth monitoring tools to identify the top bandwidth consumers and take steps to manage their usage.

Exercises

1. Use mtr to trace the route to a website or server and analyze the output for any signs of bottlenecks (high latency, packet loss).
2. Use iperf to measure the bandwidth between two computers on your network and identify any links or devices that are limiting the throughput.
3. If you have access to a network monitoring tool, explore its features for monitoring network performance and identifying bottlenecks.
4. Research common causes of network bottlenecks and learn how to address them.

By mastering the skill of identifying network bottlenecks, you can optimize your network performance, improve user experience, and ensure that your network resources are being used efficiently.

9.3 Automating Troubleshooting Tasks

Troubleshooting network problems can often involve repetitive tasks, like checking connectivity, analyzing logs, or restarting services. By automating these tasks with Bash scripts, you can save time and effort, improve consistency, and even proactively address issues before they impact users.

Why Automate Troubleshooting?

- Save Time and Effort: Automating repetitive tasks frees up your time to focus on more complex issues or proactive network management.
- Improve Consistency: Scripts ensure that troubleshooting steps are performed consistently every time, reducing the risk of human error.
- Proactive Problem Solving: You can schedule scripts to run periodically and automatically detect and address potential problems before they escalate.

- Faster Response Times: Automated troubleshooting can help you respond to network issues more quickly, minimizing downtime and reducing the impact on users.
- Documentation and Reporting: Scripts can automatically generate reports and logs of troubleshooting activities, providing valuable documentation for future analysis or auditing.

Tasks You Can Automate

Here are some common network troubleshooting tasks that you can automate with Bash scripts:

- Connectivity Checks: Regularly check the connectivity to critical servers, websites, or network devices. If a connection fails, the script can send an alert or even attempt to automatically restore the connection.
- Log Analysis: Parse log files to identify error messages, suspicious activity, or performance issues. The script can filter, extract, and analyze log data, and then generate reports or trigger alerts based on the findings.
- Service Restarts: If a service is down or unresponsive, a script can automatically attempt to restart it.
- Network Configuration Changes: You can automate network configuration changes, such as updating DNS settings, modifying firewall rules, or changing interface configurations, in response to specific events or conditions.
- Performance Testing: You can automate performance testing using tools like iperf or mtr to regularly measure network throughput, latency, and packet loss.

Example: Automated Connectivity Check and Restart

Bash

```bash
#!/bin/bash

host="www.critical-server.com"
```

```bash
service="apache2"

# Check if the host is reachable

if ping -c 4 $host > /dev/null 2>&1; then

  echo "$host is reachable"

else

  echo "$host is unreachable. Attempting to
restart $service..."

  sudo systemctl restart $service

  echo "Service $service restarted."

fi
```

This script checks the connectivity to a critical server. If the server is unreachable, it attempts to restart the Apache web server.

Example: Automated Log Analysis and Alerting

```bash
Bash

#!/bin/bash

logfile="/var/log/auth.log"

# Extract failed SSH login attempts

failed_logins=$(grep "Failed password" $logfile |
grep "sshd" | wc -l)

# Send an alert if there are more than 5 failed
login attempts

if (( failed_logins > 5 )); then
```

```
  recipient="admin@example.com"

  subject="Security Alert: Multiple failed SSH
logins"

  message="There have been $failed_logins failed
SSH login attempts. Please investigate."

  echo "$message" | mail -s "$subject"
"$recipient"

fi
```

This script analyzes the authentication log file (auth.log) and sends an email alert if there are more than 5 failed SSH login attempts.

Example: Automated Performance Testing with iperf

Bash

```
#!/bin/bash

server="192.168.1.10"

logfile="iperf_results.log"

# Run iperf and capture the output

iperf -c $server -t 30 >> $logfile

# Analyze the output for bandwidth and latency

# ...
```

This script runs iperf to measure the bandwidth between the current machine and a remote server and appends the results to a log file.

Real-World Examples

- Automated Failover: You can create a script that monitors the connectivity to your primary internet connection and automatically switches to a backup connection (e.g., a cellular modem) if the primary connection fails.
- Self-Healing Networks: You can write scripts that automatically detect and address common network problems, such as restarting services, clearing caches, or adjusting network settings.
- Security Monitoring and Response: You can automate the analysis of security logs and trigger alerts or automated responses (like blocking IP addresses) when suspicious activity is detected.

Exercises

1. Write a Bash script that checks the connectivity to your default gateway and restarts your network interface if the gateway is unreachable.
2. Write a Bash script that analyzes a web server error log and sends an email alert if specific error messages are found.
3. Create a Bash script that runs iperf periodically to monitor the bandwidth of your internet connection and logs the results.
4. Research tools like fail2ban and psad and learn how to integrate them with Bash scripts for automated security monitoring and response.

9.4 Resolving Common Issues

Even with the best network monitoring and troubleshooting tools, you'll inevitably encounter situations where your network throws you a curveball. But don't worry, I'm here to equip you with the knowledge and techniques to tackle those common network problems and get your network back on track.

1. No Network Connection

This is perhaps the most frustrating issue – your device can't connect to the network at all. Here's a breakdown of how to approach this:

Check Physical Connections:

- Cables: Ensure all network cables are securely plugged in at both ends (device and router/switch/wall).[1] Look for any signs of physical damage to the cables. If you have a spare cable, try swapping it out to rule out a faulty cable.
- Wireless: If you're using Wi-Fi, make sure your device's Wi-Fi is turned on and that it's connecting to the correct network.[2] Check the signal strength and try moving closer to the wireless access point if the signal is weak.

Verify Network Configuration:

- IP Address: Ensure your device has a valid IP address.[3] If you're using DHCP, try releasing and renewing the IP address using dhclient. If you have a static IP configuration, double-check that the IP address, subnet mask, and default gateway are correct.
- DNS Settings: Make sure your DNS server settings are correct. You can try using a public DNS server like Google Public DNS (8.8.8.8 and 8.8.4.4) to see if that resolves the issue.[4]

Restart the Network Interface:

Sometimes, simply restarting the network interface can resolve connectivity problems.[5] You can do this using the ip command:

```
Bash
```

```
sudo ip link set eth0 down

sudo ip link set eth0 up
```

Update Network Drivers:

Outdated or corrupted network drivers can cause connectivity issues.[6] Check for driver updates on the manufacturer's website or through your operating system's package manager.

2. Intermittent Connectivity

This issue can be particularly tricky because the connection drops in and out unpredictably. Here's how to investigate:

Wireless Interference:

- If you're using Wi-Fi, interference from other devices (microwaves, cordless phones, etc.) can cause intermittent connectivity.[7] Try changing the Wi-Fi channel on your router or moving your device closer to the access point.
- Driver/Firmware Updates: Ensure your wireless network adapter has the latest drivers and firmware.

Loose Cables:

Even a slightly loose cable can cause intermittent connectivity.[8] Check all connections and make sure they are secure.

Network Infrastructure Problems:

Intermittent connectivity can sometimes be a sign of problems with your network infrastructure, such as a faulty router, switch, or cable.[9] Try to isolate the problem by connecting your device directly to the modem or trying a different network cable.

3. Slow Network Performance

Slow network performance can have various causes. Here's how to troubleshoot it:

- Identify Bandwidth Hogs:

Use tools like iftop or bmon to identify applications or devices that are consuming excessive bandwidth. You might need to limit their usage or prioritize other applications.

- Check for Network Congestion:

Use mtr to monitor the network path to a remote host and look for signs of congestion (high latency, packet loss). If you identify congestion on a specific hop, you might need to investigate that network segment or contact your ISP.

- Upgrade Network Infrastructure:

If your internet connection is slow, consider upgrading to a faster plan. If your network hardware (router, switches) is outdated, upgrading to newer equipment might improve performance.[10]

- Optimize Application Settings:

Some applications have settings that can affect network performance. For example, you might be able to adjust the quality settings for video streaming or limit the download/upload speeds for file sharing applications.

4. Can't Reach Specific Hosts or Websites

If you can connect to the network but can't access certain hosts or websites, here's what to check:

- DNS Resolution:

Make sure your DNS settings are correct. Try using a different DNS server, such as Google Public DNS (8.8.8.8 and 8.8.4.4), to see if that resolves the issue. You can also use nslookup or dig to test DNS resolution directly.

- Firewall Rules:

Check your firewall settings to ensure that they are not blocking access to the specific host or website. You might need to add a rule to allow the traffic.

- Remote Host Status:

The problem might be with the remote host or website itself. Try accessing the resource from a different device or network to see if it's reachable. You can also use online tools to check the status of a website or server.

Exercises

1. Troubleshoot a "No Network Connection" issue on your own computer or another device.
2. If you experience intermittent connectivity, try to identify the cause and implement a solution.
3. Use mtr and iperf to diagnose a slow network performance issue.
4. Troubleshoot a problem where you can't access a specific website or server.

By understanding how to resolve these common network connectivity issues, you become a more effective network troubleshooter, capable of quickly diagnosing and resolving problems that arise in your network environment. This is a crucial skill for maintaining a reliable and efficient network for yourself or your organization.

Chapter 10: Advanced Troubleshooting Techniques

It's time to level up your troubleshooting skills and explore some advanced techniques. Think of this as becoming a network surgeon – you're going deeper, using more specialized tools and techniques to diagnose and resolve complex network problems. We'll explore packet capture and analysis, learn how to debug network services, and even write Bash scripts to automate solutions for those tricky network issues.

10.1 Packet Capture and Analysis

Packet capture and analysis is a powerful technique for troubleshooting network problems and understanding network behavior. Think of it like being a detective at a crime scene – you're carefully collecting evidence (packets) and analyzing it to reconstruct what happened and identify the culprit (the source of the network issue).

Why Capture and Analyze Packets?

- Deep Visibility: Packet capture gives you a granular view of the raw data flowing through your network. This allows you to see exactly what's happening at the network level, beyond what you might see in logs or with other monitoring tools.
- Troubleshooting Complex Issues: When faced with a tricky network problem that's hard to diagnose with standard tools, packet capture can provide the detailed information you need to pinpoint the root cause.
- Security Analysis: Packet capture is essential for security investigations. You can analyze captured traffic to detect malicious activity, identify intrusion attempts, and understand how attacks are carried out.

- Performance Optimization: By analyzing packet timings, sizes, and sequences, you can identify network bottlenecks, latency issues, and other performance problems.
- Protocol Analysis: You can use packet capture to study the behavior of different network protocols and understand how they work.

Tools for Packet Capture

- tcpdump: This command-line tool is a versatile and powerful packet sniffer. It allows you to capture network traffic based on various filters, such as:
  - **Interface:** Specify the network interface to capture on (e.g., eth0, wlan0).
  - **Host:** Capture traffic to or from a specific host (IP address or hostname).
  - **Port:** Capture traffic on a specific port (e.g., port 80 for HTTP).
  - **Protocol:** Capture traffic using a specific protocol (e.g., TCP, UDP, ICMP).
  - **Expression:** Use more complex filtering expressions to capture specific types of traffic.

Here are some examples:

Bash

```
sudo tcpdump -i eth0 -w capture.pcap  # Capture
all traffic on eth0 and save it to capture.pcap

sudo tcpdump -i wlan0 host 192.168.1.10 -nn  #
Capture traffic to/from 192.168.1.10 on wlan0

sudo tcpdump -i eth0 port 80 -nn -X  # Capture
HTTP traffic on eth0 and display it in
hexadecimal
```

- **Wireshark:** This graphical tool provides a user-friendly interface for capturing, filtering, and analyzing network traffic. It offers a wide range of features, including:
  - Live Capture: Capture packets from live network interfaces.
  - Offline Analysis: Analyze packets from previously captured files (pcap format).
  - Filtering: Filter packets based on various criteria, similar to tcpdump.
  - Packet Inspection: Inspect the contents of packets in a hierarchical format, showing the different protocol layers.
  - Protocol Decoding: Decode the contents of packets for various protocols (HTTP, DNS, SSH, etc.) to understand their meaning.
  - Statistics and Graphs: Generate statistics and graphs to visualize network traffic patterns.

Analyzing Captured Packets

Once you've captured packets, the real work begins – analyzing the data to extract meaningful insights. Here's a breakdown of what to look for:

Network Errors:

- Examine packets for error flags or unusual sequences that might indicate network problems. For example, TCP retransmissions can indicate packet loss or network congestion.
- Look for ICMP error messages, such as "Destination Unreachable" or "Time Exceeded," which can provide clues about connectivity issues.

Protocol Anomalies:

- Inspect the contents of packets to ensure they conform to the expected protocol formats. Deviations from the standard can indicate misconfigured devices, software bugs, or even malicious activity.
- For example, if you're analyzing HTTP traffic, check if the request and response headers are correctly formatted and if the data is being transmitted as expected.

Performance Issues:

- Analyze packet timings and sizes to identify potential bottlenecks or latency issues. Look for patterns of high latency, jitter (variation in latency), or large packet sizes that might be impacting performance.
- For example, if you see a significant delay between a request and a response, it could indicate a slow server, network congestion, or a problem with a specific network link.

Security Threats:

Look for suspicious patterns in the captured traffic, such as:

- Port Scans: An attacker scanning your system for open ports.
- Unauthorized Access Attempts: Repeated failed login attempts or attempts to access restricted resources.
- Malware Communication: Traffic patterns that match known malware signatures or communication with suspicious IP addresses.

Tips for Effective Packet Analysis

- Use Filters: Use filters in tcpdump or Wireshark to capture only the traffic that is relevant to your troubleshooting. This will make the data more manageable and easier to analyze.
- Focus on Key Protocols: Familiarize yourself with the common network protocols (TCP, UDP, HTTP, DNS, SSH,

etc.) so you can understand the contents of the packets and identify any anomalies.

- Look for Patterns: Look for patterns in the captured traffic, such as repeated connection attempts, unusual port activity, or high volumes of traffic from specific sources.
- Correlate with Other Data: Correlate your packet analysis with other information, such as system logs, network monitoring data, and user reports, to get a complete picture of the problem.

Real-World Examples

- Troubleshooting Application Issues: You can capture traffic between an application and a server to diagnose communication problems or identify performance bottlenecks.
- Identifying Network Intrusions: You can use packet capture to detect and analyze network intrusion attempts, such as port scans, denial-of-service attacks, or attempts to exploit vulnerabilities.
- Analyzing VoIP Call Quality: You can capture VoIP traffic to analyze the quality of voice calls and identify any issues with jitter, latency, or packet loss that might be affecting call quality.

Exercises

1. Use tcpdump to capture traffic on your network interface and filter it to display only HTTP traffic.
2. Use Wireshark to capture traffic and analyze a specific TCP conversation between your computer and a web server.
3. Use Wireshark to analyze a packet capture file and identify any network errors or suspicious activity.
4. Research common network attacks and learn how to use tcpdump or Wireshark to detect them.

10.2 Debugging Network Services

Debugging network services is an essential skill for any network administrator. Think of network services as the engines that drive many of the applications and functionalities we rely on – web servers, mail servers, DNS servers, file servers, and more. When these services malfunction, it can cause disruptions to business operations, communication, and user productivity.[1] Debugging these services is like being a mechanic for your network, identifying and fixing the problems that prevent these engines from running smoothly.

Why Debug Network Services?

- Restore Functionality: When a network service fails, debugging helps you identify the root cause and restore its functionality as quickly as possible.
- Minimize Downtime: Downtime for critical network services can be costly.[2] Effective debugging helps minimize downtime and reduce the impact on users and business operations.[3]
- Improve Reliability: By identifying and addressing the underlying causes of service failures, you can improve the overall reliability of your network services.
- Enhance Security: Debugging can help you identify security vulnerabilities or misconfigurations in network services that might be exploited by attackers.
- Gain Deeper Understanding: The process of debugging often leads to a deeper understanding of how network services work and how they interact with other components of your network.

Common Causes of Network Service Problems

- Configuration Errors: Incorrect or incomplete configuration settings can prevent a service from starting or functioning correctly.

- Resource Exhaustion: A service might fail if it runs out of resources, such as memory, CPU, or disk space.
- Network Connectivity Issues: Problems with network connectivity, such as DNS resolution failures or firewall restrictions, can prevent a service from communicating with other devices.
- Software Bugs: Bugs in the service's software can lead to unexpected behavior or crashes.
- Hardware Failures: Hardware failures, such as a faulty network card or disk drive, can also affect the operation of network services.[4]
- Security Attacks: Malicious attacks, such as denial-of-service attacks or exploits, can disrupt or disable network services.[5]

Debugging Techniques

Here's a breakdown of common techniques for debugging network services:

1. Check Logs:
   - Service-Specific Logs: Most network services maintain log files that record events, errors, and warnings. Start by checking these logs for clues about the problem. For example, a web server log might contain error messages indicating a missing configuration file or a failed database connection.[6]
   - System Logs: System-level logs, such as /var/log/syslog or /var/log/messages, can also contain valuable information about service failures or system-wide issues that might be affecting the service.
2. Examine Configuration Files:

Carefully review the service's configuration files to ensure they are correct and complete. Look for syntax errors, missing parameters, or incorrect values that might be causing the problem. For example, if your web server is not starting, check its configuration file (httpd.conf for Apache, nginx.conf for Nginx) for errors or missing directives.

3. Use Network Tools:
   - telnet: This command allows you to connect to a service on a specific port and send raw commands.[7] This can be useful for testing if the service is listening on the correct port and responding to basic requests.
   - nc **(netcat)**: This versatile tool can be used for similar purposes as telnet, but it also offers more advanced features, such as the ability to transfer files or listen for connections.
   - curl: This command is specifically designed for interacting with web services.[8] You can use it to send HTTP requests and analyze the responses from the server.

4. Inspect Process Status:
   - ps: This command lists running processes.[9] You can use it to check if the service's processes are running and to get their process IDs (PIDs).
   - top: This command provides a dynamic real-time view of system processes, including CPU usage, memory usage, and other metrics.[10] You can use it to see if the service is consuming excessive resources or if it's stuck in a loop.

5. Analyze Network Traffic:
   - tcpdump: This command-line tool allows you to capture and analyze network traffic between the client and the server.[11] This can help you identify communication problems, such as dropped packets, incorrect sequencing, or protocol errors.
   - Wireshark: This graphical tool provides a more user-friendly way to capture and analyze network traffic.

6. Enable Debugging Mode:

Many network services have debugging modes that provide more verbose logging and information. This can be helpful for identifying the source of the problem. Check the service's documentation for how to enable debugging mode.

Example: Debugging a DNS Server

If your DNS server is not resolving names correctly, you might:

1. Check the DNS server's log files for error messages.
2. Use dig or nslookup to query the DNS server and see if it's responding correctly.
3. Examine the DNS server's configuration files for any misconfigurations or missing zone definitions.
4. Use tcpdump or Wireshark to capture and analyze DNS traffic to see if the queries and responses are being exchanged correctly.

Exercises

1. Choose a network service (e.g., SSH, HTTP, FTP) and try to deliberately introduce a configuration error. Then, use debugging techniques to identify and fix the error.
2. Use telnet or nc to connect to a network service on a specific port and send a simple request. Analyze the response from the server.
3. Use tcpdump or Wireshark to capture and analyze the network traffic between a client and a server for a specific network service.
4. Research how to enable debugging mode for a network service of your choice and analyze the debug output.

10.3 Scripting Solutions for Complex Problems

While manual troubleshooting can be effective for simple issues, complex network problems often require a more sophisticated approach. Bash scripting allows you to automate troubleshooting steps, combine different tools and techniques, and even create self-healing mechanisms that can automatically resolve issues before they escalate.

Why Script Solutions for Complex Problems?

- Automation: Scripts can automate complex sequences of troubleshooting steps, saving you time and effort.
- Consistency: Scripts ensure that troubleshooting procedures are executed consistently every time, reducing the risk of human error.
- Proactive Response: You can schedule scripts to run periodically and proactively address potential problems before they impact users or applications.
- Flexibility: Bash provides the flexibility to combine various tools and techniques, allowing you to create custom solutions for specific network problems.
- Documentation: Scripts serve as documentation of your troubleshooting procedures, making it easier to share knowledge and reproduce solutions.

Examples of Scripted Solutions

Here are some examples of how you can use Bash scripting to solve complex network problems:

1. Automated Network Failover

Imagine you have a critical server that needs to be highly available. You can use a Bash script to monitor the server's connectivity and automatically switch to a backup connection if the primary connection fails.

```bash
#!/bin/bash

primary_interface="eth0"

backup_interface="wlan0"

gateway="192.168.1.1"

server_ip="192.168.1.10"

# Check if the server is reachable via the
primary interface

if ! ping -c 4 $server_ip -I $primary_interface >
/dev/null 2>&1; then

  echo "Server is unreachable via
$primary_interface. Switching to
$backup_interface..."

  # Bring up the backup interface

  sudo ip link set dev $backup_interface up

  # Configure the default route via the backup
interface

  sudo ip route add default via $gateway dev
$backup_interface

  # Optionally, send an alert

  # ...
```

```
fi
```

This script checks if the server is reachable through the primary interface. If not, it brings up the backup interface and configures the default route accordingly.

2. Automated Log Analysis and Remediation

You can write scripts that analyze log files for specific error messages or patterns and then take corrective action automatically.

Bash

```bash
#!/bin/bash

logfile="/var/log/syslog"

error_pattern="critical process failed"

# Check for the error pattern in the log file

if grep -q "$error_pattern" $logfile; then

   echo "Critical error detected. Restarting the
service..."

   # Restart the service

   sudo systemctl restart critical-service

   # Optionally, send an alert

   # ...

fi
```

This script checks the system log for a critical error message. If the error is found, it restarts the affected service.

3. Dynamic Firewall Rule Management

You can use Bash scripts to dynamically adjust firewall rules based on network events or conditions.

Bash

```bash
#!/bin/bash

# Get the IP address that triggered an intrusion
detection alert

attack_ip=$(grep "intrusion attempt"
/var/log/security.log | awk '{print $11}')

# Block the IP address using firewalld

sudo firewall-cmd --permanent
--add-rich-rule='rule family="ipv4" source
address="$attack_ip" drop'

sudo firewall-cmd --reload

echo "Blocked IP address: $attack_ip"
```

This script extracts the IP address from a security log that triggered an intrusion detection alert and then uses firewalld to block that IP address.

4. Network Performance Optimization

You can write scripts that monitor network performance and automatically adjust settings or configurations to optimize performance.

Bash

```bash
#!/bin/bash
```

```
threshold="100"  # Latency threshold in
milliseconds

# Measure latency to a critical server

latency=$(ping -c 4 www.critical-server.com |
tail -1 | awk '{print $4}' | cut -d '/' -f 2)

# If latency is high, switch to a different DNS
server

if (( latency > threshold )); then

  echo "High latency detected. Switching to a
faster DNS server..."

  sudo resolvectl dns eth0 1.1.1.1 1.0.0.1

fi
```

This script measures the latency to a critical server. If the latency exceeds a threshold, it switches to a different DNS server that might provide faster name resolution.

Real-World Examples

- Self-Healing Networks: Telecommunication companies use scripts to automate network diagnostics and recovery, allowing their networks to automatically identify and resolve problems without human intervention.
- Automated Security Response: Security information and event management (SIEM) systems use scripts to automate responses to security events, such as blocking malicious IP addresses or isolating compromised systems.
- Cloud Infrastructure Management: Cloud providers use scripts to automate the deployment, scaling, and management of their network infrastructure.

Exercises

1. Write a Bash script that monitors the connectivity to your internet service provider (ISP) and sends an SMS alert if the connection goes down.
2. Write a Bash script that analyzes a server's log file for error messages and automatically restarts the server if specific errors are found.
3. Create a Bash script that dynamically adjusts firewall rules based on the time of day, allowing certain services only during specific hours.
4. Research network automation tools and frameworks, such as Ansible or Puppet, and explore how they can be used with Bash to automate complex network tasks.

By mastering the art of scripting solutions for complex network problems, you can automate troubleshooting, improve network reliability, and enhance your network security.

Chapter 11: Network Security with Bash

Let's discuss network security and how you can leverage the power of Bash to fortify your defenses. Think of Bash as your security toolbox, filled with scripts and commands that can help you harden your systems, detect intrusions, perform security audits, and automate essential security tasks.

11.1 Security Hardening

Security hardening is a critical process for protecting your network and systems from attacks. Think of it like reinforcing the doors and windows of your house, installing a security system, and developing good habits to prevent burglaries. In the digital world, security hardening involves taking proactive steps to reduce vulnerabilities and make it much harder for attackers to compromise your systems.[1]

Why is Security Hardening Important?

- Reduce Attack Surface: Hardening helps you reduce the attack surface, which is the total number of potential vulnerabilities that attackers can exploit.[2] By closing off unnecessary entry points and securing your systems, you make it much harder for attackers to gain a foothold.[3]
- Prevent Unauthorized Access: Hardening helps prevent unauthorized access to your systems and data, protecting sensitive information and preventing malicious activities.[4]
- Limit Damage: Even if an attacker manages to breach your defenses, hardening can limit the damage they can cause by restricting their access and preventing them from escalating privileges.[5]

- Compliance: Many security standards and regulations require organizations to implement security hardening measures to protect sensitive data.[6]
- Peace of Mind: Knowing that you've taken proactive steps to secure your systems can give you peace of mind and increase your confidence in your network's security.

Key Areas of Security Hardening

Here are some key areas to focus on when hardening your systems:

1. User and Group Management

- Strong Passwords: Enforce strong password policies that require users to create complex passwords with a mix of uppercase and lowercase letters, numbers, and symbols.[7] You can use the passwd command to set password requirements, such as minimum length, password aging, and password complexity rules.
- Lock Unused Accounts: Disable or remove any user accounts that are no longer needed.[8] Unused accounts can be vulnerable to attacks if they have weak passwords or default settings.[9]
- Restrict Root Privileges: The root account has complete control over the system, making it a prime target for attackers.[10] Limit the use of the root account and grant users only the necessary privileges to perform their tasks.[11] You can use sudo to grant specific users limited root privileges.

2. Service Management

Disable Unnecessary Services: Identify and disable any services that are not essential for your system's operation.[12] This reduces the attack surface and minimizes potential vulnerabilities.[13] You can use systemctl to manage services:

```
Bash

# List all running services

systemctl list-unit-files | grep enabled

# Disable a specific service

sudo systemctl disable --now
unnecessary-service.service
```

- Change Default Ports: Many network services use well-known default ports (e.g., port 22 for SSH, port 80 for HTTP).[14] Change these default ports to make it harder for attackers to find and exploit them. You'll need to update your firewall rules accordingly.
- Restrict Network Access: Use firewalls (iptables or firewalld) to restrict network access to services. Allow connections only from trusted IP addresses or networks.

3. File System Security

- Set Proper Permissions: Use the chmod command to set appropriate permissions on files and directories. This ensures that only authorized users and processes can access sensitive data.
- Use Immutable File Attributes: For critical system files, use the chattr command to set immutable attributes. This prevents them from being modified or deleted, even by the root user.

```
Bash

sudo chattr +i /etc/passwd  # Make /etc/passwd
immutable
```

- Regularly Check File Integrity: Use tools like tripwire or aide to monitor file integrity and detect unauthorized changes. These tools create a baseline of your system's files and then periodically compare the current state of the files against the baseline, alerting you to any modifications.[15]

4. System Updates

- Keep Your System Up to Date: Regularly update your operating system and software packages to patch security vulnerabilities.[16] Use your distribution's package manager (apt for Debian/Ubuntu, yum for Red Hat/CentOS) to install updates:

Bash

```
sudo apt update && sudo apt upgrade -y  # Update
Debian/Ubuntu
```

- Enable Automatic Updates: Configure your system to automatically install security updates to ensure you have the latest patches.[17]

Real-World Examples

- Web Server Hardening: Hardening a web server might involve disabling directory listings, configuring strong access controls, and implementing security headers like HTTP Strict Transport Security (HSTS).
- SSH Server Hardening: Hardening an SSH server might involve disabling password authentication, enabling key-based authentication, and restricting access to specific users or IP addresses.[18]
- Database Server Hardening: Hardening a database server might involve enforcing strong passwords, encrypting

sensitive data, and limiting network access to the database.[19]

Exercises

1. Review the security settings on your own computer or server and identify any areas that could be hardened.
2. Write a Bash script that disables unnecessary services on your system.
3. Use chattr to set immutable attributes on critical system files.
4. Research security auditing tools like Lynis and learn how to use them to identify vulnerabilities.

11.2 Intrusion Detection

Intrusion detection is an aspect of network security. Think of intrusion detection as the burglar alarm for your network. It's a system that constantly monitors your systems and network for signs of unauthorized access, malicious activity, or suspicious behavior. By detecting intrusions early on, you can take action to stop attacks, minimize damage, and protect your valuable data.

Why is Intrusion Detection Important?

- Early Warning System: Intrusion detection systems act as an early warning system, alerting you to potential security breaches before they escalate into major incidents.
- Proactive Security: Instead of just reacting to attacks after they've happened, intrusion detection allows you to be proactive and stop attacks in their tracks.
- Threat Awareness: Intrusion detection systems can help you understand the types of threats your network is facing and identify vulnerabilities that need to be addressed.
- Incident Response: When an intrusion is detected, the information provided by the intrusion detection system can

be invaluable for incident response, helping you investigate the attack, contain the damage, and recover quickly.

- Compliance: Many security standards and regulations require organizations to implement intrusion detection systems to protect sensitive data.

Types of Intrusion Detection Systems

- Network Intrusion Detection Systems (NIDS): These systems monitor network traffic for suspicious patterns, such as known attack signatures, anomalies, or policy violations. They are typically deployed at strategic points in the network, such as the perimeter or critical segments.
- Host-Based Intrusion Detection Systems (HIDS): These systems monitor activity on individual hosts, such as servers or workstations. They look for suspicious processes, file changes, system calls, or other signs of compromise.
- Log-Based Intrusion Detection Systems (LIDS): These systems analyze log files from various sources, such as operating systems, applications, and security devices, to identify suspicious events or patterns.

Intrusion Detection Tools and Techniques

Bash provides access to several tools and techniques for intrusion detection:

- **psad** (Port Scan Attack Detection): This tool analyzes firewall logs (iptables) to detect port scans, which are often a precursor to more serious attacks. psad can alert you to potential reconnaissance attempts and even automatically block suspicious IP addresses.
- **fail2ban:** This tool monitors log files (such as SSH logs, web server logs, or mail server logs) for signs of malicious activity, such as repeated failed login attempts or brute-force attacks. It can automatically block IP addresses that exhibit this behavior, preventing further attacks.

- Intrusion Detection Systems (IDS): Tools like Snort or Suricata are powerful open-source NIDS that can analyze network traffic for patterns that match known attack signatures or anomalies. They can be configured to generate alerts, log events, or even block traffic in real-time.
- Log Analysis: You can write Bash scripts to analyze system and application logs for suspicious events, such as:
    - Failed login attempts: Look for repeated failed logins, especially from unfamiliar IP addresses.
    - Unauthorized access attempts: Monitor logs for attempts to access restricted files or directories.
    - Unusual file activity: Detect unusual file modifications, deletions, or creations, which might indicate malware activity.
    - Suspicious process execution: Identify processes running with elevated privileges or processes that match known malware signatures.

Example: Analyzing SSH Logs for Suspicious Activity

Bash

```bash
#!/bin/bash

logfile="/var/log/auth.log"

# Extract failed SSH login attempts from the last hour

grep "Failed password" $logfile | grep "sshd" |
grep "$(date -d '1 hour ago' '+%b %e')"

# Count the number of failed attempts from each IP address

grep "Failed password" $logfile | grep "sshd" |
awk '{print $11}' | sort | uniq -c | sort -rn
```

This script extracts failed SSH login attempts from the authentication log and then counts the number of failed attempts from each IP address. This can help you identify potential brute-force attacks.

Real-World Examples

- Detecting Malware Infections: A HIDS might detect a malware infection by identifying suspicious file activity or process execution on a host.
- Preventing Brute-Force Attacks: fail2ban can be used to block IP addresses that repeatedly try to guess passwords for SSH, FTP, or other services.
- Identifying Network Reconnaissance: A NIDS like Snort can detect port scans or other reconnaissance activity that might indicate an attacker is gathering information about your network.

Exercises

1. Install psad and configure it to monitor your firewall logs for port scans.
2. Set up fail2ban to protect your web server from brute-force attacks.
3. Research open-source NIDS like Snort or Suricata and learn how to configure them to detect specific types of attacks.
4. Write a Bash script that analyzes your web server logs for suspicious activity, such as access to sensitive files or unusual user agent strings.

11.3 Security Audits

Security audits is a practice for maintaining a strong security posture in your network. Think of a security audit as a comprehensive health checkup for your network's security. It's like having a security expert come in and thoroughly inspect your systems, configurations, and practices to identify any weaknesses or vulnerabilities that could be exploited by attackers.

Why Conduct Security Audits?

- Identify Vulnerabilities: Security audits help you identify vulnerabilities in your systems, configurations, and security practices that you might have overlooked.[1]
- Assess Risk: Audits help you assess the risk associated with these vulnerabilities, allowing you to prioritize remediation efforts based on the potential impact.[2]
- Meet Compliance Requirements: Many industries and regulations require regular security audits to ensure compliance with security standards and protect sensitive data.[3]
- Improve Security Posture: By identifying and addressing weaknesses, security audits help you improve your overall security posture and reduce the risk of successful attacks.[4]
- Increase Awareness: Audits raise awareness of security issues among your team and promote a security-conscious culture.[5]

Types of Security Audits

- Vulnerability Assessments: These audits focus on identifying vulnerabilities in your systems and applications.[6] They often involve using automated vulnerability scanning tools to detect known weaknesses.[7]
- Penetration Testing: These audits involve simulating real-world attacks to test the effectiveness of your security controls and identify vulnerabilities that could be exploited by attackers.[8]
- Configuration Audits: These audits review the configuration of your systems and network devices to ensure they comply with security best practices and policies.[9]

- Compliance Audits: These audits assess your compliance with specific security standards and regulations, such as PCI DSS, HIPAA, or ISO 27001.[10]

Bash Tools for Security Audits

Bash provides access to several tools that can be used for security audits:

- **Lynis:** This open-source security auditing tool performs a comprehensive scan of your system, checking for vulnerabilities in various areas, including user accounts, file permissions, network configuration, and installed software.[11] It provides a detailed report with recommendations for hardening your system.
- **chkrootkit:** This tool checks for signs of rootkits, which are malicious programs that attackers use to gain unauthorized access to systems and hide their presence.[12]
- **rkhunter:** This is another rootkit detection tool that scans for known rootkits and suspicious files. It also checks for common security misconfigurations.
- **Bash Scripts:** You can write your own Bash scripts to automate security checks, such as:
  - Verifying file permissions: Check if sensitive files and directories have appropriate permissions.[13]
  - Checking for open ports: Identify open ports on your system and verify that only necessary services are listening.[14]
  - Auditing user accounts: Review user accounts, groups, and password policies to ensure they comply with security requirements.[15]
  - Analyzing log files: Analyze log files for suspicious activity or security events.[16]

Example: Running a Security Audit with Lynis

```bash
Bash

# Download and run Lynis

wget https://cisofy.com/files/lynis-$(lynis
--version).tar.gz

tar xvfz lynis-*.tar.gz

cd lynis

sudo ./lynis audit system
```

This will run a comprehensive security audit of your system and generate a detailed report with recommendations for improvement.

Example: Checking for Open Ports with nmap

```bash
Bash

# Scan for open ports on your system

sudo nmap -sT localhost
```

This command uses nmap to perform a TCP connect scan on your local system, identifying open ports and the services running on them.

Example: Auditing User Accounts with a Bash Script

```bash
Bash

#!/bin/bash

# List all user accounts

awk -F: '{print $1}' /etc/passwd
```

```
# Check for accounts with empty passwords

awk -F: '$2 == "" {print $1}' /etc/shadow
```

This script lists all user accounts on the system and then checks for accounts with empty passwords, which are a security risk.

Real-World Examples

- Compliance Audits: Companies that handle credit card information must comply with the Payment Card Industry Data Security Standard (PCI DSS),[17] which requires regular security audits to ensure the protection of cardholder data.[18]
- Vulnerability Assessments: Organizations regularly perform vulnerability assessments to identify and remediate security weaknesses in their systems and applications before they can be exploited by attackers.[19]
- Penetration Testing: Companies often hire security professionals to conduct penetration tests to simulate real-world attacks and identify vulnerabilities that might be missed by automated scans.[20]

Exercises

1. Run a security audit on your own computer or server using Lynis. Analyze the report and implement the recommendations to harden your system.[21]
2. Write a Bash script that checks for common security misconfigurations, such as weak passwords or unnecessary services.[22]
3. Research different types of security audits and their specific purposes.
4. Learn about security standards and regulations that are relevant to your industry or organization.

11.4 Automating Security Tasks

Automating security tasks with Bash is a way to enhance your network's security posture. You see, managing network security can be a time-consuming and repetitive process. But with Bash scripting, you can automate many of these tasks, freeing up your time, improving consistency, and even proactively addressing security threats. Think of it like having a tireless security robot working 24/7 to protect your network.

Why Automate Security Tasks?

- Efficiency: Automation saves you time and effort by handling repetitive security tasks, allowing you to focus on more strategic security initiatives.
- Consistency: Scripts ensure that security tasks are performed consistently and accurately every time, reducing the risk of human error.
- Proactive Security: You can schedule automated security tasks to run regularly, proactively identifying and addressing vulnerabilities or threats before they can be exploited.
- Scalability: Automation allows you to manage security across a large number of systems or devices more efficiently.
- Improved Response Time: Automated tasks can respond to security events more quickly than manual intervention, minimizing the impact of attacks.

Security Tasks You Can Automate

Here are some examples of security tasks that you can automate with Bash scripts:

Regular Security Scans:

- Vulnerability Scanning: Use tools like nmap with vulnerability scanning scripts (NSE) to automatically scan your systems for known vulnerabilities.
- Security Auditing: Schedule regular security audits using tools like Lynis to identify weaknesses in your system configuration.
- Malware Scanning: Use command-line antivirus tools like ClamScan to regularly scan your systems for malware.

Log Monitoring and Alerting:

- Analyze Logs: Write scripts that parse log files (system logs, application logs, security logs) to identify suspicious activity or security events.
- Generate Alerts: Send alerts via email, SMS, or messaging platforms when suspicious events are detected.
- Trigger Automated Responses: Configure scripts to take automated actions, such as blocking IP addresses or disabling services, in response to specific events.

Security Hardening:

- Disable Unnecessary Services: Automate the process of disabling unnecessary services to reduce the attack surface.
- Configure Firewalls: Use scripts to configure and update firewall rules, ensuring that only authorized traffic is allowed.
- Manage User Accounts: Automate user account management tasks, such as creating new accounts, enforcing password policies, and disabling inactive accounts.

Incident Response:

- Isolate Compromised Systems: Write scripts that can automatically isolate compromised systems from the network to prevent further damage.
- Collect Forensic Evidence: Automate the collection of forensic evidence, such as log files, network traffic captures, and system snapshots.

Example: Automated Vulnerability Scanning

```Bash
#!/bin/bash

# Scan for vulnerabilities on a web server

nmap -sV --script vuln www.example.com
```

This script uses nmap with the -sV flag for version detection and the --script vuln option to run vulnerability scanning scripts against a web server.

Example: Automated Log Analysis and Alerting

```Bash
#!/bin/bash

logfile="/var/log/auth.log"

# Check for failed SSH login attempts

failed_logins=$(grep "Failed password" $logfile |
grep "sshd" | wc -l)

# Send an alert if there are more than 5 failed
attempts

if (( failed_logins > 5 )); then
```

```
recipient="admin@example.com"

subject="Security Alert: Multiple failed SSH
logins"

message="There have been $failed_logins failed
SSH login attempts. Please investigate."

echo "$message" | mail -s "$subject"
"$recipient"

fi
```

This script checks the authentication log for failed SSH login attempts and sends an email alert if a threshold is exceeded.

Example: Automated Security Hardening

Bash

```
#!/bin/bash

# Disable unnecessary services

sudo systemctl disable --now telnet.service

sudo systemctl disable --now ftp.service

# Update the system

sudo apt update && sudo apt upgrade -y

# Configure firewall rules

sudo ufw allow ssh

sudo ufw allow http

sudo ufw allow https
```

```
sudo ufw enable

echo "Security hardening completed."
```

This script disables unnecessary services, updates the system, and configures basic firewall rules using ufw.

Real-World Examples

- Security Information and Event Management (SIEM) Systems: SIEM systems use automation to collect and analyze security logs from various sources, identify threats, and trigger alerts or automated responses.
- Intrusion Prevention Systems (IPS): IPS systems use automation to detect and block malicious network traffic in real-time.
- Security Orchestration, Automation and Response (SOAR) Platforms: SOAR platforms use automation to orchestrate complex security workflows, such as incident response and threat intelligence gathering.

Exercises

1. Write a Bash script that automatically scans your system for malware using ClamScan.
2. Write a Bash script that monitors your firewall logs for blocked IP addresses and sends an alert if a specific IP address is blocked repeatedly.
3. Create a Bash script that automates the process of creating new user accounts with strong passwords and limited privileges.
4. Research security automation tools and frameworks, such as Ansible or Puppet, and explore how they can be used with Bash to automate security tasks.

Chapter 12: Bash for Cloud Networking

Cloud computing has revolutionized the way we build and manage networks, offering incredible flexibility, scalability, and cost-effectiveness. But with this flexibility comes complexity. Managing cloud network resources, automating deployments, and interacting with cloud APIs can be quite a challenge. That's where Bash comes in – it provides the tools and scripting capabilities to tame this complexity and make you a cloud networking wizard.

12.1 Managing Cloud Network Resources

Managing cloud network resources isa critical skill in today's world of cloud computing. You see, cloud providers like AWS, Azure, and Google Cloud offer a vast and ever-expanding array of network resources – virtual private clouds (VPCs), subnets, virtual machines (VMs), load balancers, firewalls, and much more.[1] Managing these resources effectively is essential for building, scaling, and securing your applications and services in the cloud.[2]

Why Manage Cloud Network Resources?

- Control and Flexibility: Managing cloud network resources gives you fine-grained control over your network environment.[3] You can define your network topology, configure IP address ranges, control access to resources, and customize your network to meet your specific needs.
- Security: Proper management of network resources is crucial for security. You can use security groups, firewalls, and access control lists (ACLs) to protect your cloud resources from unauthorized access and threats.[4]
- Scalability and Performance: Cloud networking allows you to scale your network resources up or down as needed to

meet changing demands.[5] Effective management ensures that your network can handle growth and maintain optimal performance.[6]

- Cost Optimization: By managing your network resources efficiently, you can avoid unnecessary costs and optimize your cloud spending.
- Automation: You can automate many cloud network management tasks, saving time and effort while ensuring consistency and reliability.[7]

Bash and Cloud Command-Line Interfaces (CLIs)

Each major cloud provider offers a command-line interface (CLI) that provides a powerful way to interact with their services.[8] And the good news is that you can use Bash to script these CLIs and automate many of your cloud network management tasks.

- **AWS CLI:** The AWS CLI provides a comprehensive set of commands for managing virtually every aspect of Amazon Web Services (AWS), including:[9]
  - VPCs and Subnets: aws ec2 create-vpc, aws ec2 create-subnet, aws ec2 describe-vpcs
  - EC2 Instances: aws ec2 run-instances, aws ec2 start-instances, aws ec2 terminate-instances
  - Security Groups: aws ec2 create-security-group, aws ec2 authorize-security-group-ingress
  - Load Balancers: aws elb create-load-balancer, aws elb register-instances-with-load-balancer
  - And many more: The AWS CLI covers a wide range of AWS services, including storage, databases, and management tools.[10]
- **Azure CLI:** The Azure CLI provides commands for managing Microsoft Azure resources, including:[11]
  - Virtual Networks: az network vnet create, az network vnet list
  - Virtual Machines: az vm create, az vm start, az vm delete

- Load Balancers: az network lb create, az network lb rule create
- Network Security Groups (NSGs): az network nsg create, az network nsg rule create
- And more: The Azure CLI covers various Azure services, including storage, databases, and app services.[12]
- **Google Cloud CLI (gcloud):** The gcloud CLI provides commands for interacting with Google Cloud Platform (GCP) services, including:[13]
  - Virtual Private Clouds (VPCs): gcloud compute networks create, gcloud compute networks subnets create
  - Compute Engine Instances: gcloud compute instances create, gcloud compute instances start
  - Firewall Rules: gcloud compute firewall-rules create, gcloud compute firewall-rules list
  - Load Balancers: gcloud compute backend-services create, gcloud compute url-maps create
  - And more: The gcloud CLI covers a wide range of GCP services, including storage, databases, and Kubernetes Engine.[14]

Example: Creating an AWS Security Group with Bash

```bash
Bash

#!/bin/bash

group_name="my-security-group"

description="Allow SSH and HTTP access"

# Create the security group

aws ec2 create-security-group \

    --group-name $group_name \
```

```
    --description "$description" \

    --vpc-id vpc-0xxxxxxxxxxxxxxxxx   # Replace
with your VPC ID

# Allow SSH access from anywhere

aws ec2 authorize-security-group-ingress \

    --group-name $group_name \

    --protocol tcp \

    --port 22 \

    --cidr 0.0.0.0/0

# Allow HTTP access from anywhere

aws ec2 authorize-security-group-ingress \

    --group-name $group_name \

    --protocol tcp \

    --port 80 \

    --cidr 0.0.0.0/0
```

This script uses the AWS CLI to create a security group with rules allowing SSH (port 22) and HTTP (port 80) access from any IP address.

Scripting Cloud Network Management

You can use Bash scripts to automate various cloud network management tasks:

- Create and manage VPCs and subnets: Define your network topology, configure IP address ranges, and control network access between different parts of your cloud environment.[15]
- Launch and configure virtual machines: Launch VMs with specific operating systems, instance types, storage options, and security settings.
- Manage security groups and firewalls: Control network access to your cloud resources, allowing or blocking traffic based on rules you define.[16]
- Configure load balancers: Distribute traffic across multiple VMs to ensure high availability and fault tolerance.[17]
- Automate backups and snapshots: Regularly back up your cloud resources to protect your data and ensure business continuity.[18]
- Monitor cloud resources: Use cloud monitoring APIs or tools to collect performance metrics and send alerts if there are any issues.[19]

Real-World Examples

- Automated Infrastructure Deployment: Companies use Bash scripts to automate the deployment of their cloud infrastructure, ensuring consistency and reducing manual effort.[20]
- Dynamic Scaling: Scripts can be used to automatically scale cloud resources up or down based on demand, optimizing costs and performance.[21]
- Security Hardening: Scripts can automate security hardening tasks, such as configuring firewalls, applying security patches, and enforcing strong password policies.

Exercises

1. Install the AWS CLI, Azure CLI, or Google Cloud CLI and explore their commands for managing network resources.[22]
2. Write a Bash script that creates a VPC and a subnet in your preferred cloud environment.

3. Write a Bash script that launches a virtual machine with a specific operating system and security group.
4. Use the cloud CLI to configure a load balancer that distributes traffic across two virtual machines.

12.2 Automating Cloud Deployments

Automating cloud deployments is a game-changer in cloud computing. You see, deploying applications and services in the cloud can be a complex process, involving many steps – provisioning infrastructure, configuring networks, installing software, and managing dependencies. Doing this manually can be time-consuming, error-prone, and difficult to scale. That's where automation comes in, and Bash can be your automation superhero.

Why Automate Cloud Deployments?

- Speed and Efficiency: Automation significantly speeds up the deployment process, allowing you to get your applications and services up and running faster.
- Consistency and Reliability: Automated deployments ensure that your infrastructure and applications are deployed consistently every time, reducing the risk of human error and configuration drift.
- Scalability: Automation makes it easier to scale your deployments, whether you need to deploy to multiple environments, regions, or cloud providers.
- Reduced Costs: Automation can help you optimize your cloud resources and reduce costs by avoiding manual errors and ensuring efficient resource utilization.
- Improved Collaboration: Automated deployments promote collaboration among developers, operations teams, and security teams by providing a consistent and transparent deployment process.

Bash and Cloud Deployment Tools

Bash can be used with various cloud deployment tools and techniques:

- Cloud Provider CLIs: You can use the command-line interfaces (CLIs) provided by cloud providers (AWS CLI, Azure CLI, gcloud CLI) to script and automate deployments. These CLIs offer a wide range of commands for provisioning and managing cloud resources.
- Infrastructure as Code (IaC): IaC tools like Terraform and CloudFormation allow you to define your infrastructure in code, making it easier to manage, version control, and automate deployments. You can use Bash to interact with these tools, generate configuration files, and execute deployment commands.
- Configuration Management Tools: Tools like Ansible, Chef, and Puppet can be used to automate the configuration of your servers and applications. You can integrate Bash scripts with these tools to perform specific tasks or customize configurations.
- Containerization: Containerization technologies like Docker and Kubernetes simplify application deployment and management. You can use Bash scripts to build Docker images, deploy containers, and manage Kubernetes clusters.

Example: Automating an AWS Deployment with the AWS CLI

Bash

```
#!/bin/bash

instance_type="t2.micro"

image_id="ami-0c94855ba95c574c8"   # Replace with
your desired AMI ID
```

```bash
key_pair_name="my-keypair"         # Replace with
your key pair name

security_group_id="sg-0xxxxxxxxxxxxxxxxx"         #
Replace with your security group ID

user_data_script="user_data.sh"  # Script to run
on the instance

# Launch the EC2 instance

aws ec2 run-instances \

    --image-id $image_id \

    --instance-type $instance_type \

    --key-name $key_pair_name \

    --security-group-ids $security_group_id \

    --user-data file://$user_data_script
```

This script uses the aws ec2 run-instances command to launch an
EC2 instance. It also includes a user_data script that will be
executed on the instance after it's launched. This user_data script
can contain Bash commands to install software, configure settings,
or perform other tasks.

Example: Deploying a Web Server with Terraform and Bash

Bash

```bash
#!/bin/bash

# Initialize Terraform

terraform init
```

```
# Apply the Terraform configuration

terraform apply -auto-approve

# Get the public IP address of the web server

public_ip=$(terraform output -raw public_ip)

echo "Web server deployed. Public IP address:
$public_ip"
```

This script initializes a Terraform project, applies the configuration defined in your Terraform files (which would include resources like a VM, a network interface, and a security group), and then retrieves the public IP address of the deployed web server.

Real-World Examples

- Continuous Integration/Continuous Deployment (CI/CD): Companies use Bash scripts in their CI/CD pipelines to automate the building, testing, and deployment of applications to the cloud.
- Automated Infrastructure Provisioning: Scripts can automate the provisioning of cloud infrastructure, such as VPCs, subnets, and security groups, ensuring consistency and repeatability.
- Blue/Green Deployments: Bash scripts can be used to orchestrate blue/green deployments, where a new version of an application is deployed alongside the existing version, and traffic is gradually switched over to the new version.

Exercises

1. Write a Bash script that launches a virtual machine in your preferred cloud environment and installs a specific software package on it.

2. Use Terraform or CloudFormation to define a simple web server infrastructure and write a Bash script to deploy it.

3. Research different deployment strategies (blue/green, canary) and learn how to implement them using Bash scripts.

4. Explore containerization technologies like Docker and Kubernetes and how they can be used with Bash to automate cloud deployments.

12.3 Working with Cloud APIs

Cloud APIs are a way to interact with cloud services programmatically. You see, cloud providers like AWS, Azure, and Google Cloud offer APIs (Application Programming Interfaces) that allow you to access and manage their services using code. This opens up a world of possibilities for automating tasks, integrating cloud services with your applications, and building custom solutions. And guess what? Bash, combined with the right tools, can be your key to unlocking the power of these APIs.

Why Use Cloud APIs?

- Automation: Cloud APIs allow you to automate a wide range of tasks, such as provisioning resources, configuring services, collecting data, and managing your cloud infrastructure.
- Integration: You can use APIs to integrate cloud services with your own applications, websites, or scripts. This allows you to leverage cloud capabilities, such as storage, databases, or machine learning, without having to manage the underlying infrastructure.
- Customization: Cloud APIs give you the flexibility to build custom solutions tailored to your specific needs. You can create scripts or applications that interact with cloud services in unique ways.

- Programmatic Control: APIs provide a programmatic way to interact with cloud services, allowing you to manage your cloud environment using code instead of manual clicks and configurations.
- Extensibility: Cloud providers are constantly adding new features and services to their APIs, giving you access to the latest cloud innovations.

Bash and Cloud APIs

Bash, combined with tools like curl and jq, can be used to interact with cloud APIs effectively.

- **curl:** This command-line tool is your Swiss Army knife for making HTTP requests. You can use it to send API requests to cloud services, including GET, POST, PUT, and DELETE requests.
- **jq:** This command-line JSON processor is invaluable for working with API responses, which are often in JSON format. You can use jq to extract specific data, filter results, and transform JSON data.

Example: Retrieving a List of AWS EC2 Instances

Bash

```bash
#!/bin/bash

# Replace with your AWS access key ID and secret
access key

aws_access_key_id="AKIAXXXXXXXXXXXXXXXX"

aws_secret_access_key="xxxxxxxxxxxxxxxxxxxxxxxxxx
xxx"

region="us-east-1"

# Get a list of EC2 instances
```

```
instance_data=$(curl -s
"https://$region.ec2.amazonaws.com/?Action=Descri
beInstances" \

    -H
"X-Amz-Credential:$aws_access_key_id/$(date
+%Y%m%d)/$region/ec2/aws4_request" \

    -H "X-Amz-Date:$(date -u +"%Y%m%dT%H%M%SZ")"
\

    -H "X-Amz-SignedHeaders:host" \

    --user
$aws_access_key_id:$aws_secret_access_key)

# Extract instance IDs using jq

instance_ids=$(echo $instance_data | jq -r
'.DescribeInstancesResponse.reservationSet[].inst
ancesSet[].instanceId')

echo "Instance IDs:"

echo "$instance_ids"
```

This script uses curl to make an API call to the AWS EC2 service to retrieve a list of instances. It then uses jq to extract the instance IDs from the JSON response.

Authenticating API Requests

Cloud APIs require authentication to ensure that only authorized users or applications can access and manage resources. Common authentication methods include:

- API Keys: You can generate API keys that are used to authenticate your requests.

- Access Tokens: You can obtain access tokens using OAuth 2.0 or other authentication protocols.
- IAM Roles: In cloud environments, you can use IAM (Identity and Access Management) roles to grant permissions to applications or services.

Working with API Documentation

Each cloud provider provides detailed documentation for their APIs, including:

- API Endpoints: The URLs you need to use to access different services.
- Request Parameters: The parameters you can include in your API requests.
- Response Formats: The format of the data returned by the API, usually JSON or XML.
- Authentication Methods: The supported authentication methods for the API.
- Code Examples: Code examples in various programming languages to help you get started.

Real-World Examples

- Automating Cloud Security: You can use APIs to automate security tasks, such as rotating access keys, applying security patches, or monitoring for suspicious activity.
- Building Dynamic Cloud Infrastructure: You can create scripts that dynamically adjust your cloud infrastructure based on demand, scaling resources up or down as needed.
- Integrating with DevOps Pipelines: You can integrate API calls into your DevOps pipelines to automate the deployment and management of cloud-based applications.
- Creating Custom Dashboards: You can use APIs to retrieve data from cloud services and create custom dashboards to monitor your cloud environment.

Exercises

1. Research a cloud API that interests you (e.g., AWS S3, Azure Storage, Google Cloud Compute Engine).
2. Review the API documentation and understand the authentication requirements.
3. Write a Bash script that makes an API call to retrieve data from the service.
4. Use jq to extract specific information from the API response.

By mastering the use of cloud APIs with Bash, you gain a powerful tool for automating cloud management tasks, integrating cloud services with your applications, and building custom solutions. This opens up a world of possibilities for leveraging the flexibility and scalability of cloud computing.

Conclusion

You've reached the end of your journey through "Command the Network: A Practical Guide to Master Network Configuration, Monitoring, and Troubleshooting with Bash Scripts." We've covered a lot of ground, from the fundamentals of Bash scripting and networking concepts to advanced techniques for automation, security, and cloud management.

By now, you should have a solid understanding of how to leverage the power of Bash to:

- Automate network configuration tasks: Manage network interfaces, configure routing and DNS, and control firewalls with ease.
- Monitor network health and performance: Track bandwidth usage, check connectivity, monitor performance metrics, and detect anomalies.
- Troubleshoot network problems effectively: Diagnose connectivity issues, identify bottlenecks, and resolve common problems.
- Enhance network security: Implement security hardening measures, detect intrusions, perform security audits, and automate security tasks.
- Manage cloud network resources: Interact with cloud services, automate deployments, and work with cloud APIs.

While this book has provided a comprehensive foundation, the world of networking and Bash scripting is constantly evolving. Here are some ways to continue your learning and stay ahead of the curve:

- Practice, Practice, Practice: The best way to solidify your skills is to practice regularly. Experiment with different

Bash commands, write your own scripts, and explore new tools and techniques.

- Stay Curious: The world of technology is always changing. Stay curious, read blogs and articles, attend conferences, and explore new technologies.
- Contribute to the Community: Share your knowledge and experience with others. Contribute to open-source projects, write blog posts, or participate in online forums.
- Embrace Automation: Look for opportunities to automate more tasks in your network environment. Automation can save you time, improve efficiency, and reduce errors.
- Stay Secure: Network security is an ongoing process. Stay informed about the latest threats and vulnerabilities and continuously update your security practices.

Bash is a powerful and versatile tool that can be used for much more than just network management. You can use it to automate system administration tasks, process data, build applications, and much more. As you continue your journey with Bash, you'll discover its endless possibilities and its ability to simplify and automate complex tasks.

Thank you for joining me on this journey through the world of Bash for network management. I hope this book has empowered you with the knowledge and skills to command your network with confidence and efficiency. Now go forth and automate!